# ONLY JESUS

## A VOICE THAT SOUNDS LIKE HOME

## MARK HALL

PASTOR AND LEAD SINGER OF

### CASTING CROWNS

with TIM LUKE

✝ LIFESONG
PUBLISHING®

# CONTENTS

# LEGACY
## ACTS 20:24

**I FELT MY EYBROWS RISE** as I reread the paragraph, making sure I understood the writer correctly the first time.

Sure enough, he wrote what I thought he wrote.

*Does he really believe this? How can he think this way?*

Several years later, I can still see the lines on the page. The article appeared in a popular Christian publication and was written by a prominent voice respected throughout the music industry for many years. He caught my attention with his assertion that Contemporary Christian music essentially is bad art. But then he floored me when he contended that it would not last long and would leave no real legacy in music.

My frustration grew as I discussed his opinion with my managers, Norman Miller and Mike Jay. No legacy? How could he say that?

I don't remember all the secular artists he named, but he pointed out how bands like the Beatles, the Eagles, and U2 had built legacies that the world will remember forever. Such legacies won't happen in Christian music, he claimed.

"Check out what he's saying," I said before reading the paragraph to Norman and Mike.

They listened and slowly nodded before Norman said, "Yeah, it's really sad he feels that way."

"No, no, no," I said. "That's not what I mean. It's not sad that this guy thinks Contemporary Christian music won't last and no one is memorable enough."

"Of course Christian music will leave a legacy," Mike said, without hearing me. He started naming artists who had been around for years and who would always be remembered. I knew he was right. Several Contemporary Christian artists—Petra, Steven Curtis Chapman, dc Talk, and others—already have left lasting imprints.

Still, what I heard in the writer's words was not what everybody else was hearing.

"My problem isn't with his opinion. He may be wrong or he may be right with what he's saying, but who cares?" I said. "My problem with what he's saying is this: How in the world could he be in Christian music this long and still think we're here to leave a legacy and make a name for ourselves?"

Norman and Mike stared at me. Their eyebrows lifted too. Their lips said nothing, but their look said, *What are you talking about?*

I broke the silence.

"What is remembering me going to do for anybody

when all is said and done?" I asked. "I spend most of my time onstage trying to prove to the crowd that I'm more of a train wreck than they are. Their having one more person to look up to isn't going to help them."

I probably went on for another five minutes. All I know is that the writer's words have never left me. I've never quite grasped how someone so immersed and influential in Christian music for so long ever thought we're supposed to make a name for ourselves and leave a legacy.

We're not here to be remembered. We're here for the only name worth remembering. Only Jesus. That's why we're here.

\*\*\*

THE WORLD TELLS ME to be Somebody with a capital S. I *have* to be Somebody. I *must* be Somebody. We live our lives to build a resume. We tell people who we are by sharing our job titles. We talk about making names and leaving legacies, all of it for our own benefit and glory, and we wonder why it leaves our lives shallower than our graves.

All of us are tempted to chase the world's definitions of success and meaning. God knows this, so his first instruction to us is to put no gods before him. He knows that without him the biggest god in our lives will look a lot like the image we see in a mirror. Only when I open God's Word am I refocused. I can try to chase my heart's desire and make a name the world remembers—as long as I forget that my heart is so deceitfully wicked that no one can truly know it (Jeremiah 17:9).

I'm convinced that no hero in the Bible got up in the morning and thought, *I want to be a hero.* No real hero ever sets out to be one. Not only was it not their goal, but the thought probably never entered their minds because most heroic actions involve life-changing pain or danger. Mary had no idea God was preparing her to be the mother of Jesus. She was just living life and loving God. She wasn't thinking, *I want to be awesome and known around the world for all time.*

> **No real hero ever sets out to be one. Not only was it not their goal, but the thought probably never entered their minds because most heroic actions involve life-changing pain or danger.**

David had no idea when he took lunch to his brothers on the battlefield that he also would fell Goliath and save Israel. He was just going through his day and doing what his dad told him to do.

Trace the life of Abraham: He told lies and took shortcuts to achieve what he thought was best, and all along God worked around and through his shortcomings to bless the world. It seems like all the true heroes of the Bible were reluctant in some way. Even for those who launched upon what they knew were gigantic endeavors, it's like they innately still knew the secret, and the secret is this:

*I've got nothing. I have no business being here.*

The notion of not leaving a legacy so contradicts everything in our flesh that the mortal self recoils at the thought.

*How dare someone suggest that my name not be remembered! I'm important!*

The Apostle Paul says he considers his life of no value to himself (Acts 20:24) and all of his impressive worldly titles and accomplishments as rubbish (Philippians 3:8). That level of humility is the difference in a life lived for today and one that echoes through eternity.

The greatest challenge for Christians is to center our hearts on the atonement of the Cross of Christ. The atonement part was handled by Christ at Calvary. The faithfulness and obedience parts are where we stumble. Wrapped in the finite, we cannot keep our intimacy and confidence in Christ as limitless as his atonement. Instead of being content to be still in God, we feel the pulse of the world around us and chase its definitions of success. Everything in our culture screams for us to deify ourselves, to elevate the individual, to glorify ourselves as our own greatest end.

This book examines various stages of this great struggle. When I set out to write an album, I don't intentionally develop overarching themes. Yet it still happens. Every album I've written includes common themes threaded through various songs—themes I never intended and only noticed sometime during the process or after it was finished.

"Only Jesus" is all about God constantly reaching out to rescue us from our insatiable drive to find satisfaction and meaning in what the world promises, as opposed to what Jesus has already done. In particular, the story of the prodigal son (Luke 15:11-32) surfaces in several songs. I didn't intend it, but one song features the prodigal son, another features the prodigal's father, and another features the prodigal's elder brother. I pray the truths upon which these songs and book chapters are written pierce your heart for inspiration, instruction, encouragement, and, where needed, life change.

Jonathan Gess is the football coach at my church's academy. Before every Friday night game, he sends his coaching staff a text to tell them he is praying for them. His text before the region championship game last season redirected everyone's attention. He wrote: "God doesn't care if we win tonight. He doesn't care about your worldly success. He doesn't care if you are great in the eyes of the world. He cares that he is great in your eyes!"

All the kingdoms built, all the trophies won, will crumble into dust when it's said and done. All that truly matters is whether I live God's truth to the ones I love and before those to whom he leads me. Is my life proof that there is only one whose name will last forever?

It took a while for me to get there, but I've come to the conclusion that I don't want to leave a legacy. I don't care if people remember me. I've only got one life to live, and after seeing my share of mountaintops of success and valleys of heartaches, I've resolved to let every second of it point not to myself but to him.

Only Jesus.

## Chapter 2

Listen: Nobody

# HUMBLED
### JOHN 1:19-27; 1 CORINTHIANS 3:5-8

**HE STOOD AT A DISTANCE AT FIRST.** I could tell he was reluctant, but, sure enough, he started walking toward me. Thankfully, this wasn't a real-life episode of *The People of Walmart*. He seemed like a regular guy who was harmless enough and had a slight, knowing smile on his face.

Casting Crowns has been around for a while, so I'm recognized in public from time to time. I can tell when someone really wants to say something to me, like this guy in Walmart. Most people are nervous when they meet somebody they admire. I tend not to walk up to people I look up to because I know I'm going to say something stupid, like, "You're awesome. Thanks for being awesome!"

So I have a soft spot in my heart for people in that situation. It's hard to know what to say. The guy in Walmart was a little sheepish from the start.

"Man, your music has really done a lot in my life," he said.

"Thanks, man," I said.

"There's this one song that really helped me in my faith and moved me closer to God."

And then his face went blank. Deer in headlights.

"Umm. It's umm…I think it's called…."

He couldn't remember the name of the song. He had worked up the courage to approach me, he sincerely had a fondness for one my songs, and he'd gotten past his opening line, and then…

"Umm."

*Awkwaarrrd.*

"It was about God and how much he loves us," he said.

"Uh-huh," I said, thinking, *OK, well, that's probably a lot of them.*

"Is it 'Who Am I'?" I asked.

"Nah. That's not it."

*Ouch.* That stung me a little.

He lowered his head and squinted his eyes. "It said something about the wind and stuff like that," he said.

"'Praise You in This Storm'?" I asked.

"No, no, no."

*Strike Two….*

I thought, *I'm not going to help this guy anymore. He's slaying all of my songs. It's like he's saying, "Not that old thing. That's old news." I'll just let him figure this out.*

He thought and stared and rubbed his chin and tried to come up with the song.

Finally, I couldn't take the discomfort any longer and threw out another song title.

"'Voice of Truth?'" I said.

He was shaking his head before I got out the word "Truth."

*I have no idea what song he's talking about*, I thought, and then reminded myself how tough it is to approach someone who is in the public eye.

He finally threw up his hands.

"Man, I can't remember what song it was. I just know that it was at a time when I really needed to trust God with my life in some big ways, and that song pushed me over the edge. I finally let go and trusted him. I looked up the verses that you listed with the song in the liner notes of your CD, and that's why I am who I am now."

Since I was still stuck on the fact that he couldn't remember this song from a monumental time in his life, I barely heard his last few meaningful sentiments.

I offered him polite thanks. As he walked away, I felt a strange flush of emotions and had one prevailing thought....

\*\*\*

JOHN THE BAPTIST POINTED to Jesus from the womb. He has one leg up on the rest of us. No one else can say that. Someone may be able to boast, "I was four years old when I sang a solo in my church," but John jumped up and down in his mother's womb when Mary walked into the room while pregnant with Jesus. From Day One, John pointed to Jesus and devoted his whole life to his Messiah (Luke 1:39-45).

Then came a day when society noticed John.

In John 1:19-28, priests and other church leaders approach John and ask, "Who are you? We know you're talking about this guy named Jesus. But who are *you*?" They even ask if he is Elijah (who never died but was taken to heaven by a whirlwind).

John has the chance to make a name for himself. Elvis didn't exist back then, but prophets like Moses and Elijah were as rock star as it gets. The religious leaders are giving John a chance to stake his claim in the world.

Not only does John refuse the opportunity, but he doesn't even tell them his name. He says, "I'm nobody. I'm just a voice." When you think about what he's really saying, he doesn't allow himself anything. He won't let them walk away with any knowledge about him because he gets it. His life is a flashing neon sign with an arrow pointing to Jesus Christ, and he unabashedly proclaims: "There's a gravity to what's going on right now, and a point needs to be made, but it's not me."

I joke around on social media with a series of parody videos called "Cool Dad." I say things like, "I work too hard. I care too deeply. These are my weaknesses." Notice I said "parody," because anytime someone asks us who we are in real life, we don't joke around about that. Most of us are ready with our lists. We can tell you who we are, what we've done, and how long we've been doing it.

John the Baptist has that same opportunity on a public stage. "Just tell us who you are. Are you Elijah?" Flattery is a great shortcut to get into someone's head. But if you live by that sword, you need it until you die by it. John refused even to flirt with it. I want to be like John.

My goal is to be a nobody. The world tells me I need to be a Somebody, but Scripture elevates the nobody. The one Somebody in the entire universe created us for his purposes, and if my purposes are for his glory, then I cannot be self-seeking or vain for glory.

> **My goal is to be a nobody. The world tells me I need to be a Somebody, but Scripture elevates the nobody.**

I learned something while recording the album *Only Jesus*. Even after nearly three decades of teaching Scripture, it never hit me until I was writing the song "Nobody" that we are constantly telling ourselves to stay humble. We memorize humility verses like Philippians 2:3-11 and remind ourselves to consider others more important than ourselves and to look not to our own interests but to the interests of others. We tell ourselves to have the mind of Christ and to let our attitudes be like that of Jesus.

As I considered the lyrics of this song, it hit me: All these years I've prayed for God to help me stay humble, but that prayer is never prayed by anybody who encountered Jesus after the Resurrection. Think about how Mary Magdalene, Peter, Thomas, James, Jude, and Paul responded to the risen Lord. James and Jude were his brothers who thought he was crazy during his ministry (Mark 3:21). Yet after his resurrection, they wrote epistles in which they called themselves his bondservants. They had rejected him during his ministry but called themselves his *slaves* after his resurrection. The people who walked around with the risen Jesus never had to humble themselves. They were humbled. They got it. In his presence, they felt his glory and their inadequacy.

When those religious leaders walked up to John the Baptist in a huff, the thought of humbling himself never crossed John's mind. He was already humbled because he knew who had invaded his world. His response couldn't help but drip humility: "No, no, no, you don't understand. I am nobody. I have absolutely nothing to offer you. Jesus, though? You need to meet him. He's the one. I can give you nothing."

> **The people who walked around with the risen Jesus never had to humble themselves. They were humbled. They got it.**

I'm glad you bought this book. I hope you find encouragement and inspiration in it. But it won't remove one scintilla of your sin. What else am I going to do— teach you how to sing? What's that going to do for you? Am I going to teach you how to draw or to speak publicly? I'm pretty decent at those things, too, but they won't give you new life. I can teach you how to change a tire or play or a piano. What does it all mean in comparison to eternity? When our eyes open to who Jesus is, our eyes then open to who we are, and we grasp the contrast. Everybody in the Bible who came to that realization hit the ground every time. Their response was, "You, you, you, oh Lord. Only you. I'm so sorry. Don't even look at me. I don't even deserve to be in your presence."

Yet even after a humbling event, it's amazing how quickly we get up after a few days and puff out our chests again and say, "Well all right, what are *we* going to do today, Jesus?" The more time you spend with Jesus, the less you have to humble yourself because the more you're just humbled.

The Apostle Paul lived a humbled life. Notice I didn't write "humble life." I wrote the word "humbled." He was one of those people who had been in Christ's presence, and it drove him to his knees. So he wrote passages like 1 Corinthians 2: "I was with you in weakness and in fear and much trembling, and my speech and my message were not in plausible words of wisdom, but in demonstration of the Spirit and of power, so that your faith might not rest in the wisdom of men but in the power of God" (Vv. 3-5).

His humility is more evident earlier in the passage, where he says: "I decided to know nothing among you except Jesus Christ and him crucified."

It wasn't that Paul came to them without wise and persuasive words because he didn't have them. He had them.

He was sharp. He could debate the debaters. He quoted philosophers back to them. If you read Paul's background in Philippians 3:4-6, he was at the top of the Pharisaical org chart. He wasn't saying, "I came to you in weakness because I was weak." Instead, he said, "I *decided* to elevate Christ above myself. I'm coming to you in weakness because my strength is not enough. There is an end to where I can take you and what I can do for you in my own strength."

When I get onstage, I see that truth now more than ever. If all I do is show you a funny guy who sings well and writes good songs, what can you do with that? There's nowhere to take that. It just gives you one more person on your list of someone you'll never be.

But Paul said, "I boast in my weakness, and Christ's power rests on me. So I'm going to boast all the more gladly about my weakness" (2 Corinthians 12:9).

I'm learning from Paul's example. The more I show people who I truly am, scars and all, the more they understand that it requires the grace of an almighty God to use someone like me. Paul said, "You do know I was the scum of the Earth, right? If sin had a city, I'd be the mayor" (1 Timothy 1:15).

He made such statements because he knew how quickly people want heroes. At other times, he said, "Look, some of you are deciding you're Paul's people or you're Apollos's people, and that's error" (1 Corinthians 3:4-9). At first, it seems Paul is defending himself because it hurt his feelings that some people favored another teacher. But that's not the case. He merely points out that he and Apollos are only regular people through whom God is spreading the gospel. One planted. Another watered. But God gave the growth and gets the glory. Both men are fallen but redeemed. Both are limited. But both are also surrendered and subscribe to Paul's goal in Philippians 3:7–8:

"Whatever gain I had, I counted as loss for the sake of Christ. Indeed, I count everything as loss because of the surpassing worth of knowing Christ Jesus my Lord. For his sake I have suffered the loss of all things and count them as rubbish, in order that I may gain Christ."

\*\*\*

MY PASTOR, TIM DOWDY, dropped a truth bomb during a sermon not long ago.

"Do you really think the people in your life are here just to know *you*?" he said.

I sat there dumbfounded. That thought, phrased that way, had never crossed my mind. The message was clear. If you belong to Jesus, your purpose is not to be known but to do the John the Baptist thing and point to Jesus.

Today's generations hear a question like the one my pastor asked and scoff, "Who do you think you are? I am an individual of my own choosing. You can't even assign me a gender now. You can't tell me anything. I tell you who I am."

Paul and other New Testament writers want us to

question the logical end of that line of thinking. I love my family and friends, but what do I really have for them? For all the people with whom you go to school, work, play, and even church—all the people in your circle—do you think God put you in that circle just so they can know everything about you? Or is it possible that God placed you in that circle and on that team and in that class and in that workplace so they can come to know *him*?

In the October 26 entry of his 1935 devotional book *My Utmost For His Highest*, Scottish Missionary Oswald Chambers writes, "The source of our inspiration in our service for God is behind us, not ahead of us. The tendency today is to put the inspiration out in front—to sweep everything together in front of us and make it conform to our definition of success. But in the New Testament the inspiration is put behind us, and is the Lord Jesus Himself. The goal is to be true to Him—to carry out *His* plans."

In other words, Chambers says, God isn't necessarily preparing us for some great work in the future. God is more concerned that we prepare others with the news of his great work in the past at the Cross of Christ.

So when the guy at Walmart couldn't remember my song and walked away without ever identifying it, I battled a few emotions, some selfish. But then everything that matters crystallized into focus.

He couldn't remember the name of a song that he says God used to help transform his life. We spend hours and weeks and months and sometimes years making these songs, and it'd be easy to get a little proud of what we do. I just spent a year making the *Only Jesus* album. It was the longest, hardest, most stressful time I've ever endured to create music.

Confidentiality prevents me from giving the details of walking through brutal tragedies in some of our church families and people close to me. But they left deep scars. Shortly after those haunting ordeals, right before I was scheduled to start recording the album, someone broke into my car and stole several items. The most valuable was my personal journal containing all of my thoughts and lyrics that ultimately, through the grace of God, became songs on the album. Only with the Lord's help could I start from scratch and remember most of what I had written.

In the middle of it all, I can honestly say I spiraled into a dark place that took a while to escape.

I came through so much to produce this record that it would be easy to make it a little bit more about my message than about the One to whom the message points. And I can see how, on a bad day, I could've gotten a little offended at Mr. Walmart and thought, *How can this guy not remember a song that he says was so important to him, after I put years of my life into it?*

It seems silly as I write about it now, but it's amazing how quickly we can turn inward and focus on ourselves. In those times, I have to redirect my heart away from myself and pray, "God, let me hear you in just the right way and show me your great truth."

Here's the great truth he wanted me to hear:

"You are not the point. You are here to point to the point."

That's what John the Baptist knew. That's what Paul knew. That's what we all must come to realize. Maybe God allowed my journal to be stolen because he wanted urgency in me, a focus on him that I haven't had in a while. Maybe he knew that the only way the songs would have any meaning whatsoever was if I was desperate for him.

**I realize I'm only a small part of the story God is weaving in the lives of people around me.**

I realize I'm only a small part of the story God is weaving in the lives of people around me. Only God can change someone's life. I'm just a guy who got to tell one of the stories that helped this fellow in Walmart along God's way.

At our concerts, I see thousands of people who come for a pit stop. They're running their race, and I see my place in that. The concert is just one event in their walk with Jesus. I'm a part of their night. They're not coming to mine. They have stepped out of their race for a few hours, and God lets me be a part of that moment. I ask myself: What am I going to do with those two hours?

People often say, "Your lyrics are hard-hitting and straight to the point."

All I can think is, *Dude, the fact that you're going to listen to me for four minutes, in this day and age, amazes me.* I'm flabbergasted that anybody would give me four minutes of his or her time, and if you're going to give me four minutes, I'm not going to let you leave wondering what I had to say. I'm going to get to it because of the urgency of the matter. People are desperate for hope and truth.

I am not only ordinary, I'm less than ordinary. I want to do what Paul did. I want to boast all the more gladly in my weaknesses so Christ's power can rest on me. In the first 20 minutes of our concerts, the crowd is going to know that I have dyslexia and attention deficit disorder and that I attended Learning Disabled classes in school. They're going to know that I've done dumber things since I was saved than I did before I was saved, that I'm falling down constantly, and that the Lord still stays with me. He's still uses me despite of the mess that I am.

Now, when we sing "Only Jesus" at the end of the night, I ask, "What do you know about me so far tonight? Let's make a list: Can't read. Doesn't pay attention. LD classes. Messes up everything. Forgets the words to his own songs. What else do you know about me? What else do you *need* to know about me? Your being impressed with anybody on this stage doesn't do anything for you. The only one who lasts is Jesus. The only one who will be there for you and stay with you and lift you up is Jesus."

Little by little, I understand more and more that I'm not the point but I'm here to point to the point. God has put me in these places and in these circles—the people I work with, the people I meet, the people in my family—strictly for his purposes. Surely the end of all those relationships is not just so they can know more about me. God gave me those relationships to make him known. So I've got to put me down, and I've got to lift him up.

If that sounds familiar, it's because I borrowed it. Like the Walmart guy, I couldn't remember exactly where it came from. So, I had to look it up. A fellow named John the Baptist says it in John 3:30.

"He must increase, but I must decrease."

He wasn't talking about any old nobody like himself. He was pointing to only Jesus.

# Feel It In Your Bones
## Luke 15:11-19

**Before Melanie and I had kids,** a dentist friend from church invited us to join several families at his home. I remember hearing about the dentist's backyard before we were invited. Everyone talked about his kids' "play stuff." When I thought of play stuff, I envisioned the Playskool plastic basketball goal or little pedal cars or the A-frame double swing set with metal anchors that kept it from tipping over when kids swung too high. As is usually the case with rumors, all the talk was way off base.

When we reached the dentist's backyard, he didn't have play stuff. He had a Six Flags amusement park.

Before me stood a giant wooden fortress with swings, tall slides, and tunnels. The kids giggled as they sprinted to the fortress and launched with reckless abandon into every corner of the monstrosity. I was an adult and still couldn't help myself. I'd never seen anything like it. I also giggled as I scurried through the fortress, taking up most of the space in the tunnels as kids crawled over and around me. I bumped my head and scraped my knees and almost got stuck, but the only thing I got lost in was the thrill of it all. It finally dawned on me that I was the only adult outside. I was bummed to remember I needed to hang out with the adults, so I crawled out of the fortress and shuffled inside.

After a while of fulfilling my grownup obligations, I looked out the window to wistfully check on the kids. The playground was empty. I craned my neck to look all over the fortress. Not one kid, not one sound. At first I was puzzled because I knew just how amazing the outdoor castle was. Then I was alarmed because I knew just how amazing the outdoor castle was.

I hurried out the backdoor again, this time even more quickly than when I was giddy kid earlier. The stillness made no sense. Why weren't the kids playing on the fortress? Where were they?

And then I saw them.

A mix of relief and bewilderment washed over me all at once. As soon as I cleared the huge fortress enough to see the rest of the backyard, I spotted eight kids standing shoulder to shoulder against the fence along the edge of the yard. They stood near a locked gate. The taller kids stood on their tiptoes with both hands on the railing to peer over the fence. I looked beyond the fence to see what they were watching. All I saw was thick woods. The kids stared into nothing. Had they heard a noise? Seen an animal? Thrown a ball over the fence?

"What are y'all looking at?" I asked.

"We want to go into the woods!" one yelled.

"Yeah!" said another.

"The woods?" I asked.

"Yeahhhhh!!"

Now I was really dumfounded. We'd been at the house maybe a half-hour. I looked at the enormous wooden fortress, designed so creatively and full of all kinds of fun features. I couldn't help but be jealous that I didn't have such a kingdom as a child. And then I looked at the woods. Finally, I glanced again at the backs of the kids who still lined the fence, and I couldn't help but see a life lesson in the irony.

**The kids could never get back to the place where the fortress was enough.**

Here these kids had a whole new world to play in—an expensive, safe, well-conceived play paradise. Yet after only a brief period they'd grown tired of it and wandered to the fence, going as far as they could go to try something else. The woods had been there for decades but were rendered off limits by a fence and represented an even newer experience. The kids literally had turned their backs on paradise to yearn for something they couldn't have.

The kids never could get back to the place where the fortress was enough, and they didn't want to accept that the woods were off limits. I couldn't help but realize that when I looked at the kids, I looked at all of us.

\*\*\*

ALL OF US FACE THE SAME OLD temptations and the same old lies from the enemy. Satan said to Eve in the Garden of Eden, "Are you sure this is enough?" That same serpent has been in our heads ever since.

*Are you sure you have enough? Are you sure there isn't more out there?*

We all have legitimate, God-given needs, but we sin when we try to meet our needs in our ways and in our own timing. When our needs are met and we feel loved, we're fine. But as soon as that faucet doesn't flow as freely as we want, we invent ways to scratch our itches and meet our needs through whatever shortcuts we can find.

The truth is that we're not content with being nobodies. We're not content with having only Jesus. For fallen human nature, the very Savior who is all we need just simply isn't enough. I don't have much confidence in Bruce Springsteen as a theologian, but he wrote a song that nailed who we are. We're born to run, spiritual tramps with restless souls in desperate need of rescue. We're born with a nature tilted away from God, and not one is righteous on our own (Romans 3:10). In fact, our own righteousness, the very best we can muster, is as filthy rags in comparison with the holiness of God (Isaiah 64:6).

So we run. We run to our own goals, our own ideas, our own ownership. We run from submission, from surrender, from second place. We try everything we can to increase because intentionally trying to decrease is counterintuitive to everything in our nature.

The temptation of Christ in the wilderness, just before he launches his ministry, is instructive for us all. The Apostle John says the whole world is under the sway of the wicked one (1 John 5:19) and all temptation can be boiled down to the lust of the flesh, the lust of the eyes, and the pride of life (1 John 2:16). Satan tried to throw those darts at Jesus, and Satan uses those same darts on us; he just dips them in different colors and poisons based on our appetites and weaknesses. They look different, but they're not.

We often think younger generations have it easier than their predecessors. While that may be the case because of modern conveniences, I would argue that kids face more challenges now than ever. Not only is the traditional nuclear family under assault, but also temptation and worldly influences reach them more quickly. The whole world is at their fingertips. They literally can access the darkest depths of man's depravity every time they pick up their phones. But it's always the same tricks and lies that all men have faced: the lust of the flesh, the lust of the eyes, and the pride of life.

Jesus dealt with those temptations without failure and yet still became guilty of all them. God dumped the guilt and condemnation for the lust of the flesh, the lust of the eyes, and the pride of life on his Son on the Cross. Jesus Christ carried the guilt for the darkest sins we could ever conceive.

Jesus felt the pain of every sin, but he never felt the pleasure of it. He's the only one who ever felt the bite of sin but not the enjoyment of indulgence.

When I read the accounts of the Temptation of Christ in the gospels (Matthew 4:1-11; Luke 4:1-13), a few observations stand out. First, it's the ultimate Spoiler Alert. We know who's going to win. I mean, surely Jesus will say no to any temptation, right? Come on, he's God. It's like when somebody shoots at Superman in a movie. It's going to bounce off of him. Why be nervous as we watch the movie?

Remember, though, Jesus is fully God and fully man. His temptation wasn't a sham. His humanity felt every ounce of the temptations, and yet he was an overcomer for our sake. Because of him, we can now be more than conquerors:

"Since then we have a great high priest who has passed through the heavens, Jesus, the Son of God, let us hold fast our confession. For we do not have a high priest who is unable to sympathize with our weaknesses, but one who in every respect has been tempted as we are, yet without sin" (Hebrews 4:14-15).

Yet the story has a twist. While Satan launches the same temptations at Jesus that he throws at all of us—the lust of the flesh and eyes and the pride of life—he almost always tempts us with stuff we want and don't have. When Satan comes to Jesus, he offers him things that Jesus already has. Everything Satan offers Jesus could be considered good or a natural human need, and everything that he offers Jesus, oddly, is already his. This realization confused me at first. Satan knows who Jesus is. He knows he's God. He knows he's the Creator and King of the universe. Why does he offer Jesus stuff that's already his? Why would Jesus fall for that? Why would it even be considered temptation?

Then it hit me. It's a temptation because Satan offers it to Jesus *now*.

*You don't have to do the Cross. You can have all of these things now and avoid all of that agony.*

Nothing is new under the sun. Satan whispers the same message to you and me:

*You don't have to wait until you're married to do married things. You can have that now. It's a lot harder to wait. Just have it now. Why wait for God's timing?*

*Why wait to see what God's timing is on your job? Instead of working hard and waiting until your boss sees how good you are, why not take every opportunity to criticize fellow employees and tear down their reputation so you can get ahead?*

*Instead of telling the truth even to your own detriment, why not deceive to cover your tracks and cast yourself in the best light? You can have it now. Why wait?*

One of life's big temptations is to avoid difficulty, the hard route, the narrow way, and the suffering. Why persevere when you can escape? Why work for something when you can have it right now?

\*\*\*

EVERY TIME I READ THE STORY of the prodigal son in Luke 15:11-32, I think of the kids on the dentist's playground. The prodigal son enjoys a life of abundance, and he knows half of a sizeable inheritance is coming his way. The fact that he has an estate to inherit shows his family is wealthy. But waiting on half of the estate isn't good enough. He has to have it now. I see people in this place all the time—and not just sweet little kids lining a fence.

I imagine the prodigal son working in his father's field. He's drenched in sweat and has a cramp in his back. He's filthy. He's parched. He lifts his head to feel a cool breeze and notices that none of the laborers in the next field is working. Everyone is milling around, drinking cold water, and eating fruit. It's almost his break time, too, but everything looks better over there, and they're only hired workers....

*If I'm a son and all this is really mine, why do I have to do all of this hard work? It would be so freeing to have my inheritance now. That's what I want. I want what is rightfully mine, and I want it now.*

That's the lie the son fell for, and that's a lie we've all fallen for.

So the prodigal son runs. Life is good at first, but he soon squanders all his possessions on wanton living. He discovers that the boundaries and the life that his father had given him were as good as it gets. Back home, he was in the middle of everything he ever needed—only to assume he was missing out on something better. When you drill down into his motives, he wanted freedom. Freedom is a code word for control. The prodigal son wanted the reins of his own existence.

At the beginning of the story, the prodigal has all the blessings of a family that is loving and even wealthy. He knows what's coming to him, but it's not enough that his future is secure. He's more concerned about his "now." The son wants his share of the inheritance without submitting to the authority that would be in place until his father dies. In other words, when he asked his dad for his inheritance, he communicated, "I wish you were dead."

Too often we want what comes along with God but we don't really want God. We want the peace and comfort and joy. But, more than anything, we want control. The way we live shows we don't want God to control our lives, and yet we still have the audacity to wonder, "How can I get all of that peace stuff too?"

The giant lie at the end of all of our own plans is that they're still not going to take us far enough to satisfy. Usually when we're running from God, the end game is not in mind. The now is in mind. It's like watching the Epic Fail videos on social media. You see the teenager on the roof and the trampoline below him, you watch the disaster unfold, and you wonder, "What did he think was going to happen when he jumped? You have to go somewhere after hitting a trampoline that hard, and that place can't be good."

Jesus tells the story of the prodigal son so we can see

ourselves in it. The prodigal wanted the stuff of God. He just didn't want God. He wanted the stuff of family, but he valued independence over family relationships. He felt that the walls around his world were there to keep him in. He didn't realize what those walls were keeping out.

***

*Do you feel him in your heartbeat, even when you're running?*
*You try to drown him out with your life,*
*but you still hear him calling*
*With a voice you've never heard, but it sounds like home*
*You try to shut it out, but you feel it in your bones*
*And it won't leave you alone*

WHEN YOU'RE RUNNING FROM GOD, you'll still have quiet moments. God is right there in those quiet moments, still reaching out to you. Have you ever noticed that when you're running from God you'll change the radio station away from the Christian song that is speaking to you or the sermon that is convicting you? The most miserable person on earth is a believer trying to run from God. Whatever you're trying to do to run away from him, you can't keep the noise loud enough to drown him out. He won't let you—because you're his, no matter how much you want to try to be your own.

*As a kid you said your prayers, now they're bouncing off the ceiling*
*It took your world away when you trusted him for healing*
*He's no stranger to your heartbreak*
*He knows how it feels to lose*
*From the garden to the Cross, he's been chasing after you*

As a student pastor, I see people running from God every week. When a kid comes to Wednesday night worship, it's not like he stopped running when he walks into church. He's running in his chair right at that moment and doing everything he can do to drown out the truth I speak. Or she's doing everything she can do to avoid making eye contact with me.

I see it every week. They're fidgeting in their seats, they're talking to people next to them, and they're going to the bathroom three times. Their worldly influences, though they don't realize it, are making them run as fast as they can. They know innately that if they slow down and listen, they'll hear God's quiet beckoning, and if they hear it, they'll have to deal with it.

I remember enduring those nights as a young man. I would lie in bed and stare at my ceiling fan after chasing the thing I thought I wanted. I had to face the fact that it was not what I wanted at all. Yet God was still there, still loving me, still calling me.

We'll paint over the truth to avoiding facing it. We'll paint it as judgment to get away from it. We'll paint it as a "worldview" so we can rationalize it away. We'll paint it as hate speech. We'll paint it as anything we can imagine to avoid dealing with it. That's why believers must be in God's Word for ourselves. Whatever someone may say to us, we can figure out a way to discount it. But when we're alone and the room gets quiet, we know. Deep down, we know we can't discount God's truth.

> *Your fear isn't dark enough, your pit isn't deep enough,*
> *Your lie isn't loud enough to keep him away from you*
> *The Father made the way for you, the Son killed the grave for you*
> *Let his Spirit come alive in you; are you tired of running?*

Many of us have run hard enough and far enough that we thought we could never come back home. We've told ourselves, "God is gonna be finished with me."

We can never forget that nothing can separate us from the love of God (Romans 8:37-39). His love is always there. It's there right now. If you even recognize that still, small voice persistently calling out to you, it's proof that God is with you right now. His love is inescapable.

I purposely ended the song "Even When You're Running" in a way that reminds us of this truth. The song's off-the-rails music signifies the leaves slapping our faces as we're running, but then the music ends, the song gets quiet, and all that's left is a soft voice, calling out to all who will listen.

*It's time to stop running now. You don't need to have it all figured out. You just need to come home.*

True to human form, the prodigal son tries to figure out his return: "OK, I know my father surely will be judgmental and condemning. I know he won't take me back all the way. But maybe he'll take me back a little bit."

We all ask ourselves, "How am I going to make this right with God?" That line of thinking keeps us running away and believing we have no way back to him—as though we're the ones who have to come back. The lesson of the prodigal son is that it's not about our coming back. It's about our turning around from where we're headed. Jesus is already right there waiting on us.

Right there where we are. As soon as we turn around.

It's time to stop running now. You don't have to have it figured out. All you need to do is turn around. For me, turning around is the definition of the word *repent*. The prodigal son repents. He is mistaken on how his father is going to receive him, but he turns from his sinful running. That is his responsibility in this story.

God's love is inescapable. He comes after me, but I have to turn around.

Sometimes the lust of the flesh, the lust of the eyes, and

> **The lesson of the prodigal son is that it's not about our coming back. It's about our turning around from where we're headed.**

the pride of life so entangle us that it feels impossible to break free. The single hardest thing many of us will ever have to do is turn around.

Know this: The moment you turn around and repent, the Father will come running. At that moment, ironically, the only one running is the Father. Straight to you.

> *His love is inescapable, his presence is unshakable*
> *Right now you don't believe it's true; a better day's coming*
> *You don't need another place to hide; he'll find you in your darkest night*
> *His love is holding on to you…*
> *Even when you're running*

## Chapter 4

Listen: Awaken Me

# A Beautiful Thing
### Ephesians 5:14; Isaiah 6:1-6

**GROWING UP IN SOUTH ALABAMA** has its perks. While heat, humidity, and gnats seem like a curse, God is still good. The blessing is right down the road.

A few hours from my hometown of Montgomery is Panama City Beach, Florida, one of the playgrounds of the South. My memories of PCB, as we call it, are vivid. I can still hear my parents yelling for me to be careful as I sprinted across the beach and into the ocean. I couldn't wait to body surf the waves. Of course, the waves at PCB are about a foot high, but they're huge in the eyes of a kid.

One day, that water taught me a valuable life lesson.

As I swam and laughed and carried on with my sister and friends, I noticed the persistence of the waves. Over and over, they crashed me back toward the shore. What I didn't notice, at first, was a subtler phenomenon. While the waves pushed me toward the beach, the current slowly carried me sideways. I was being moved and didn't know it. I remember playing with friends and looking up to see mom. I'd see her chair and umbrella, and I'd always focus on that spot. I'd play and look up to see her again. Then I'd play a little longer and look up to see her, but this time she wasn't there. She was a little more to my left. Then I'd start playing again, riding the waves or throwing the ball back and forth. The next thing I knew—I don't know how it happened—I was 60 yards down the shore and looking for mom. The first time I experienced it, I remember standing up, rubbing salt water out of my eyes and thinking, *What just happened?*

**Satan knows our time with God is the lifeline that reminds us of truth.**

I realize this analogy is worn, but it's also personal. It reminds me of the times when I've slipped in my walk with Jesus.

When I say *slipped*, I don't mean I indulged in all the cliché sin and darkness. It was much more nuanced. It began when the enemy succeeded in chipping away my time with Jesus.

Satan knows our time with God is the lifeline that reminds us of truth. Since Satan traffics only in lies, he wants us to know as little truth as possible. The first thing he comes after in believers' lives is our time with Jesus—our time in God's Word and in prayer.

God gave us his Word because he knows our feelings are part of our fallen nature. In other words, our emotions are fallen too. They're faulty and never trustworthy, so we constantly need to remind ourselves of God's truth. He told us through the Apostle Paul in Romans, "Do not be conformed to this world, but be transformed by the renewal of your mind" (12:2). You've read that verse before, but sometimes we forget Paul's intended audience. He wrote that verse to *Christians* in Rome—believers with saved spirits but lost thinking. He implores them to constantly come back to the Word.

In Colossians Paul opens a deep theological can for believers. He lets us in on the secret that God has seated us— past tense—with Christ in the heavenlies.

This inexplicable transaction took place at your salvation and means you have a place setting in eternity. Now that you're in on the secret, he implies, you also should put your mind where Christ is, and he is seated at the right hand of the Father. You're *in* Christ, and he's seated in Heaven, so you're seated in Heaven. You're God's child and you're forgiven and justified, but part of being sanctified (set apart in holiness in an unholy world) is you have to start "thinking saved."

In effect, God says, "Here's my Word. Keep coming back to this, and I'm going to remind you who I am and who you are." Time after time I've gone back to the Word, read something that pierced through my callused heart, and said to myself, "That's right. What was I thinking?" The enemy knows this, so he wants to get me away from my Bible.

The antidote to evil is the holiness of God's Word. Satan is doing a better job than ever of bending hearts away from Scripture. We are the most distracted generation in history. I believe people around the world are more biblically illiterate than we've been in thousands of years. We at least used to give God our spare time, sad as that is. But at least most believers would read the Word in those little cracks between busyness. Now we have a phone in our pocket that fills all the cracks. We don't even spend our leftover time in God's Word. The enemy has crafted a perfect storm in which the longer we go without spending time with Jesus, the less focused we are. We don't belong to him any less, but questions that once were black and white evolve into gray.

I wrote a song about this digression called "Slow Fade" on *The Altar and the Door* album. It highlights a spiral described in Psalm 1: "Blessed is the man who walks not in the counsel of the wicked, nor stands in the way of sinners, nor sits in the seat of scoffers; but his delight is in the law of the LORD, and on his law he meditates day and night" (Vv. 1-2).

Here's a man who is walking and then standing and finally sitting. He's slowly shutting down, and the downward spiral starts with his counsel—the counsel of the wicked. If the enemy can change our counsel to worldly counsel, faithfulness gives way to compromise, and our lives will follow.

"Awaken Me" is a story too. It's a song about waking from a slow fade, looking up, and realizing I have drifted so far down the shore that I can't find home base anymore.

The song opens with music designed to mimic the spiritual slumber into which we sometimes sink. The piano slowly blends with the strings to represent those moments where

God quietly breaks through our stubbornness and says, "Where are you? What are you doing?"

The first lyric asks, "Lord, what were you saying?" It's like I'm wiping the sleep out of my eyes because I've heard a familiar voice in a foreign place.

It describes waking up from a deep sleep, the kind where your eyes won't open and then finally only one eye opens and your face is still wadded up and you're looking around the room, unsure what day it is or whether it's daytime or nighttime. Those moments happen to me when I fall asleep during the day and it turns dark while I'm asleep. I'm so disoriented that I look around and wonder, "Where am I?" It's an awful feeling.

Be assured that when we run from Jesus, he will wake us. We find ourselves hearing him ask, "Where are you?" Simultaneously, we squint through the fog of our tainted lives and answer his question with our own: "Where *am* I?"

The Lord has tried to wake me plenty of times as I ran from him, and I only wanted to roll over. I didn't want to think about it. He is jealous for his children though. He is resolute. We enjoy one source of unconditional love—only Jesus. He will escort our lives to that wakeup moment in which we finally ask, "What happened to me? How did I drift this far?" It happens only when he has softened our hearts enough to get in. And when your heart is soft like that….

Move.

Turn around.

The heart has an uncanny ability to heal itself from conviction. We can harden up again in a quick minute.

When God wakes you—and sometimes he has to shake you awake through a trial—and you realize that you're not where you're supposed to be, it's time to move. It's time to surrender.

The prodigal son in Luke 15 hit rock bottom after wasting everything his father had given him. One of the turning points of his story comes in Luke 15:17. I love the way it's phrased:

"But when he came to himself...."

It was the moment when God awakened the young man to his depravity.

> **Only Jesus can awaken us from our self-absorbed spiritual comas.**

Only Jesus can do this. Only Jesus can awaken us from our self-absorbed spiritual comas. Only the power of his Holy Spirit can give us new life when we're lost or can bring us back to him when we're already his child but running from him. Ephesians 5:13-14 compares God's truth to a bright light. Imagine being asleep in a dark room when a stark light shines directly into your eyes.

"But when anything is exposed by the light, it becomes visible, for anything that becomes visible is light. Therefore it says, 'Awake, O sleeper, and arise from the dead, and Christ will shine on you.'"

Christ, the only righteous one, does all the work. He jars

us from our apathy, and the contrast of his light against our dark ways ushers us through conviction and into repentance. When the prophet Isaiah saw a vision of heaven and felt the searing realization of God's holiness against his own depravity, he cried, "'Woe is me! For I am lost; for I am a man of unclean lips, and I dwell in the midst of a people of unclean lips; for my eyes have seen the King, the LORD of hosts'" (Isaiah 6:5)!

That Scripture inspired a lyric in the bridge of "Awaken Me:"

*"Come let your fire make holy these lips unclean. Shine down with all your glory. Awaken me."*

It is the prayer of someone once again awakened by God to the truth that we all sin and fall short of his glory. Anytime people come close to God in the Bible and understand they are in the presence of the Almighty, their reaction is always similar: "Woe is me. Just leave me. I don't deserve to be here."

The awakening moment is a convicting moment, and it's a beautiful thing. Yet we must learn to distinguish between shame and conviction. Shame drives us back to slumber. Shame says, "Just take something and roll over and go back to sleep. It's not going to get any better."

Conversely, the Holy Spirit's grace and kindness leads us to repentance in him. His conviction actually draws us to him. It doesn't chase us away. God doesn't say, "Let me jump all over you for being bad." God says, "Let me awaken you to come to me."

When we do, we are blessed when we take refuge in him, when we taste and see that the Lord is good (Psalm 34:8). He takes us to a place where we join with the psalmist to beg, "Create in me a clean heart, O God, and renew a right spirit within me. Restore to me the joy of your salvation, and uphold me with a willing spirit" (Psalm 51:10, 12). Notice that God is still the one doing the upholding even when our spirits are finally willing to obey again.

Isaiah suffered through his aforementioned stark moment in his blinding vision of a holy God, but he also tasted God and saw that he is good. We know this because of the promise God personally left Isaiah—and all of us:

"For I will not contend forever, nor will I always be angry; for the (human) spirit would grow faint before me, and the breath of life that I made…. He went on backsliding in the way of his own heart. I have seen his ways, but I will heal him; I will lead him and restore comfort to him" (Isaiah 57:16–18, parenthesis added).

## Chapter 5

Listen: Love Moved First

# GOD IS LOVE
## LUKE 15:20-24; ROMANS 5:8

**THIS IS THE STORY OF A RUNAWAY.**

His heart had grown dull even though he had been in church from the age of nine until 19. For the last few years he had run away from almost everything he had learned just so he could taste the world. A young man, a car, and a little pocket change are a dangerous combination. And sometimes the stench of the world's pigpen is disguised by designer cologne.

He was a saved believer. He would tell you that. But little else of God's truth filtered past his ears and into his heart.

Now he was holding a gun in his friend's car parked outside of a store in Montgomery, Alabama. His friend had walked into the store and left him in the passenger seat, alone with his dark thoughts and the friend's loaded handgun. All he had to do was lift the gun to his head and end it all. Then the pain would be gone.

The gun felt cold. His insides felt colder.

Thank God, the only thing that went through his head that day was a fleeting thought of what it would be like to pull the trigger. That silly thought stopped everything: He thought about his friend having to clean up the mess in his own car. And that was that.

You're holding my book, so you know that as a 19 year old I didn't kill myself. I was tempted mostly because I was in a terrible state of mind. I was at rock bottom after my girlfriend and I broke up. I discovered that when you build your life around another person and that person leaves, you don't have a life anymore.

*There's nowhere to go from here,* I thought. *There's no digging out of this. It's never going to be any better. It's never going to be any different. This is just the way life is because she was the only good thing going in my life.*

I didn't think I had anything to offer anybody. I was an artist who liked to sketch pictures. Big deal—I liked to draw. I was so distraught that I soon would flunk out of college. I worked at a little mall store, and didn't know what I wanted to do with my life. All I knew was that this girl was supposed to be the answer. We were young, and the biggest mistake of my life to that point was making her my world.

Think about it. Here's a kid from South Alabama who had lived with dyslexia, ADD, and the humiliation of Learning Disabled classes in public school. I heard all the jokes about riding the short bus. Suddenly a pretty girl actually liked me.

We started dating, and then we kept dating, and then we got serious. I envisioned engagement rings and proposals at some point. Then, suddenly, her path introduced her to guys a lot more interesting than me.

It was over. Just like that.

I knew I was a Christian. I knew God was real because I had yelled at him the night before. I sat in my car in her driveway and screamed at God that he needed to fix this mistake, because she was the one. I literally screamed at the roof of the car. In the coming days my world grew scary dark, and I didn't see any hope. I didn't see any way out and didn't want one.

When I would think about God, all that registered was I knew he was there and he loved me. More pressing, I also knew I was in a hole I dug for myself. It didn't seem possible for God to get to me. I didn't see a way to get to him.

It's crazy that I'd heard truth at church every Wednesday and Sunday since being saved at nine and still thought this way, but I did. I have no idea how it was possible for me to be in church that long and never know that life didn't rest on my shoulders. God was a backup plan in my mind. He was the one you talk to when your grandparents are sick. He was the one you turn to when you're about to go down in flames and you'll do whatever it takes, or when you're ready to go to Africa and save the world. He was warm feelings and campfire songs. I didn't have any room in my heart for anything bigger. I thought I had experienced all of God there is.

Did I mention that I was 19?

Looking at Scripture now, which is the same Bible I carried around every week most of my life, it floors me to think that the same truth that means so much to me now was right there in my hands the whole time. It's like a poor man who finds a bag of gold and still walks around begging. He has a backpack full of gold coins and somehow the windfall doesn't register with him. All he can think about is how much the backpack cramps his style. *Ugh, this stupid backpack. Thing weighs a ton.* That's the very definition of religion. It usually is rooted in knowing just enough Scripture to be dangerous to yourself and lethal to others.

The point of Scripture is not just to know Scripture. The point of Scripture is to truly *know* Jesus.

\*\*\*

IN THE DARK PERIOD AFTER THE BREAKUP with my girlfriend, I immersed myself in my passion of drawing pictures. I took Advanced Studio Art with a bunch of seniors headed to art school. I met a guy who painted with nothing but knives. One girl painted the stages of evolution on a wooden chair. The adjective *eclectic* fell short in describing this group.

Several of us liked to listen to music while we worked. I loved music and pretty much had glued headphones to my head. Every once in a while, my classmates and I would switch headphones, and the music poured so much darkness into me that it was the perfect storm when my girlfriend and I broke up. I had all the right music to kill myself with.

I also liked a Classic Rock radio station in Montgomery. Great classic tunes. But every Sunday evening, two nerdy preacher guys somehow bought 30 minutes of airtime on this Classic Rock station. I'd be drawing and rocking out and taking the "Stairway to Heaven" with Zeppelin, and the next thing I know I'd hear, "Power for Today, where we get together and read through Scripture and see how it applies to you."

The two nerdy guys would say things like, "Okay, here we are, it's 'Power for Today.' I'm John…and I'm Steven…and now we're here to look at today's Scripture and take your questions."

I remember pausing my art pen without looking up, rolling my eyes, and letting out and audible, "Ugh." But I didn't want to bother with changing the station, so I kept listening. It was churchy, but I didn't care because I went to church every Sunday, and I was curious about what these guys would say on a rock station. John and Steven would take calls from all kinds of people. I remember one lady caught my attention right away.

"Here's what's going on. I've got this job and it's really a lot of pressure, and the boss is harsh and I can't do anything about it," she said. "I have to deal with all the pressure of the way he treats me."

"Hmm, good call, Jan," Steven said. "It kind of reminds me of a Scripture in Philippians."

I remember thinking, *What does Philippians have anything to do with a dirtbag boss?*

"If you look at Philippians 1, you'll see that Paul also deals with people who don't have his best interests in mind and are even competing against him and likely saying bad things against him when he is weak and tired," Steven said. "Philippians 1:15-18 says, 'Some indeed preach Christ from envy and rivalry, but others from good will. The latter do it out of love, knowing that I am put here for the defense of the gospel. The former proclaim Christ out of selfish ambition, not sincerely but thinking to afflict me in my imprisonment. What then? Only that in every way, whether in pretense or in truth, Christ is proclaimed, and in that I rejoice.' Have you ever prayed for your boss?"

"No."

"Well, let's pray for your boss right now."

I thought, *Whaaaaaat? You want to pray for the lady's boss, the jerk in the story? You're supposed to tell us how God is going to zap him with an attitude adjustment and change his life.*

**I must let God handle those tough seasons for me.**

Steven went on to say what I've been saying for years now: I must let God handle those tough seasons for me. I've got to give it to him when somebody says harsh things about me. It doesn't mean I shouldn't stand up for myself, but I should never seek to avenge myself or bang on the walls and demand my rights to my offender. I need to back up and let God make sure my heart is right. Do I really want things to be right between the offender and me? Or do I just want him to be in trouble? If I want him to be in trouble for what he's done, maybe something's not right in my heart yet.

Steven prayed. Then the lady prayed, and they asked God to bless the boss. I wasn't drawing anymore. I stared at the radio and said out loud, "That's in the Bible?" I thought the Bible was only stories about giants and walking on water and stuff that happened thousands of years ago. It seemed like everything in the Bible never happens anymore.

I found myself gravitating to "Power for Today" each week, searching out two nerdy guys talking about God's Word and how God belongs in all of your life, not just part of it.

I had heard a lot of these truths before, but my heart wasn't ready to receive any of it. I remember listening to "Power for Today" and hoping that somebody would call with questions similar to mine. That radio show, more than anything else, prodded me to turn to God's Word for life answers. I started with the book of James because it was short and I figured that even I could stay focused long enough to understand it.

God used two Bible nerds on a rock station on Sunday afternoons to start moving toward me. Even in my darkness, when I had convinced myself there was no way out, the Lord began working his way in. God's Word is living and active, sharper than any two-edged sword. It cuts straight to the heart. (Hebrews 4:12) Just as the rain falls from the heavens and doesn't return to the heavens without feeding the earth, so is his Word that comes from his mouth. It never returns to him void. It always accomplishes what he sets forth (Isaiah 55:10-11). It was like God parachuted truth right into my little war zone. Then my dad gave me a couple of albums by Christian artists that started changing my music appetite. Little by little, God moved toward me.

God is love (1 John 4:8), and he didn't wait for me to find my way to him. I couldn't have crossed that distance even if I wanted to—and plenty of times I didn't want to. Yet he came running after me. Almost anybody else would've turned up their noses at me and left me at my worst. Not God. Not his limitless grace. Love moved first.

***

THIS IS THE STORY OF A RUNAWAY, yes; but more accurately, it's the story of a runaway's father.

After the prodigal son comes to himself in Luke 15:17, he returns toward home to beg his father to forgive him and take him back and hire him as a servant. That's when love moved first.

"But while he was still a long way off, his father saw him and felt compassion, and ran and embraced him and kissed him" (Luke 15:20).

The picture is that of a loving father who not only didn't turn away from his wayward son but also didn't even pause to ask a word about where the son had been or what he had done. He simply fell on his neck and kissed him.

His boy was home.

I know what it's like to be in the son's shoes. When I was 19 and sulking through depression after the breakup, I thought, *I don't even deserve to ask for help.* I didn't know enough theology to understand who God is. I just knew I was a loser.

Even when the prodigal wanted to go home, it never entered his mind that he would be anything more than slave. That's strange. Did his dad ever do anything to communicate that message? Certainly not, but the prodigal knew what he deserved and knew what he probably would do if the roles were reversed.

**I didn't know enough theology to understand who God is. I just knew I was a loser.**

"Well, if I was dad I'd tell you what I'd do. I'd tell my son, 'You get off my property, and maybe, just maybe, you can hang around outside of the gate for a few weeks. I'll let you know if I'm going to let you in.'"

We think the same way. We assume God is like us. We assume God loves like we love. We assume his anger is like ours. We assume his patience is like ours, and there ain't nothing more dangerous than a Christian who's right. We have power when we're right, and we fantasize of showing people exactly who we'd be if we were in control. We would rain down fire, man, and people who wronged us would be toast.

The prodigal based his picture of the father upon what

he knew he deserved and what he would do if he were the authority. He didn't see any way back to the father because the father owed him nothing. The son already had taken everything coming to him after his dad liquidated assets. He even may have put his dad in debt just to go off and do his thing. He figured his father could never forgive him and take him back without severe retribution.

When you're not in the Word for yourself, you have to figure out God by yourself. In my darkest times, I thought, *There's no way to get back to him. I've already done everything I ever learned you're not supposed to do, and I'm only 19. Good grief. It just doesn't seem like there's a way.* And that's when the hopelessness came.

At those times, we have to remember the runaway's father. When the prodigal was a long way off, the father came running. It was socially unacceptable and unmanly for men to run in Palestine. The father's actions would've left Jesus' hearers stunned and even offended as he told this story. But love doesn't care. Love always moves first.

God is willing to do anything—even send his Son to die—to build a bridge for people to reach him.

One of the songs my dad sang solo in church is called, "He Came to Me," written by Squire Parsons. It touched my heart every single time he sang the chorus: "*He came to me, when I could not come to where he was, He came to me, and that's why he died on Calvary. I couldn't come to where Jesus was. So he came to me.*"

Until I became an adult and started growing in my faith,

I always saw the Cross of Christ as something I had to go back to. Maybe it was because it was in the past. Maybe it was because it was so long ago. Maybe it was because he was so innocent and I'm so guilty, but I just didn't see how it all worked. It's weird how you can have parts of truth in your mind and they never connect, and it never really connected that God made the first move toward me.

After the first sin, God showed up in the garden and met Adam and Eve right where they were and clothed them. Then he moved toward people through judges, then kings, and always through prophets. Then he moved even closer to people when he came in the flesh in the Person of Jesus Christ. Finally, he moved even closer through his Holy Spirit who now indwells his people. He has relentlessly moved toward us.

Jesus said, "No one can come to me unless the Father who sent me draws him" (John 6:44). Scripture makes it clear that even the faith to believe in him is a gift from him (Ephesians 2:8-9). He is drawing us to him. Even after we're saved, he continues to reach out to draw us ever closer. We're not the ones who make it happen. We're not figuring out who he is on our own, and we're not realizing something new and deciding that we're going to follow him. Either God is in control or he's not. Even in our running, he is drawing us closer to him. He's the author and the finisher of our faith (Hebrews 12:2). If he begins the work, he's going to complete it (Philippians 1:6). The fact that I even know that I'm lost is only because he told me (Ephesians 2:4-5).

The Bible paints a picture of a giant hand reaching out to us. It's not waiting on us. It's reaching out to us. This source of hope assures us that life isn't all banking on us. Only Jesus is the source of that hope. That giant hand belongs to him.

One of my first misconceptions about God was that I had to unbreak myself—I had to become unbroken for God to save me. I had to get back to him. That is error. Even when we are dead in our trespasses, God forgave us. Dead people can't do anything.

Another big misconception was that after I was saved I then had to perform to maintain God's favor. Scripture opened my eyes to the truth that he's holding on to me and I'm not holding on to him. One of the first verses I memorized was, "And we know that for those who love God all things work together for good, for those who are called according to his purpose" (Romans 8:28).

Even when dark things happen, God is at work. He's always moving toward us. He's always at work for our best and for his glory.

From a grave meant to keep him to a stone rolled away, Christ's Cross is the proof that love made the first move. I remember where he found me, and I'm still amazed at the grace in which I stand. His Cross is the proof that love made the first move.

## Chapter 6

Listen: The Change in Me

# The Gentleman
### John 14:15-31

**She was so quiet.** Maybe that's one of the reasons I could hear God so well.

My wife, Melanie, and I had already chosen our next child as soon as we saw her photo from the adoption agency, but when we finally met her she didn't make a sound. And still she confirmed everything we already knew. We named her Hope because she embodied the faith God gave us in the gift of our fourth child.

When we adopted Hope, she was two-and-a-half years old and didn't talk. As little as a baby can talk at that age, she was quieter than most. Even the workers at the orphanage in China said she wasn't a talker. She sat still while most other kids frolicked with loud chatter.

A two-and-a-half year old born to English-speaking parents normally picks up a lot of words by that age, yet here we were starting from scratch with a kid who had heard nothing but Chinese. It wasn't exactly a smooth transition. When Hope wanted something, I usually could discern her request because she would point or reach for it. But when she was upset, we struggled to figure out why. She had no way to tell us, and I ached for her.

*Just tell me what it is and I'll get it. I'll do anything you want if you'll tell me what it is.*

Slowly but surely she started learning a few English words, like the word, "No." She had that one down pat in no time.

"No."

I can still hear it.

"Hope, would you like some carrots?"

"No."

"Here, Hope, let's put on this shirt."

"No."

A few other words followed in the days afterward. By the time Hope was three, she understood maybe 40 to 50 words. She knew even less about me. She knew I picked her up. She knew I sat her down, and she knew I told her no. That's it. She had a tiny bit of knowledge about me, but she could have comprehended more about me if she knew more than a few dozen words.

She couldn't understand almost everything that came out of my mouth. She had no file for it. I had to try to relate to her within her small vocabulary.

She'd point at a Chrysalis and I'd try to explain what it

is. My mouth was moving, but all she heard was noise. She knew "butterfly," and that was about it. I knew so many things to tell her about the wonder of how a caterpillar builds a cocoon around itself and transforms not only into something beautiful but something totally different. All she heard was "caterpillar...butterfly." Until her vocabulary grew, she couldn't conceive how to ask me questions, and the reason she didn't really know how to ask questions was because her biggest need was to learn how to *hear* me.

In the same way, when we spend time in God's Word, we build the vocabulary in which he is able to communicate with us. We build a base of knowledge about him that we couldn't know before—attributes that we didn't know—only as we expand our biblical vocabulary. A lot of believers get saved as a child, go to their graves, and meet Jesus having never learned more than 30 or 40 words. They never get to know him more than, "He forgave me and he saved me."

I don't want to sound for a minute like that's not a big deal. It is monumental. Still, before I devoted myself to Bible study, I spent at least half of my life in a tiny world of repeatedly saying, "Forgive me, help me. Forgive me, help me. Forgive me, help me." I didn't know anything more existed. I even had the ignorant audacity to think, *Wow, I've kind of got the Bible down now and really don't know what else it can tell me. I've read all these verses before.*

Someone would begin a devotional by saying, "Hey, we're going to look at the book of James today," and I'd think,

*Oh, I've read all of James. I studied that like a year ago. I've gotten all there is to get from that book.* More accurately, I had gotten all I could *handle* from that book. I had gotten all that God was able to say to me because I didn't have a vocabulary big enough to grasp the rest of the incredible riches in James.

The more time we spend in God's Word, the more our biblical vocabularies and our hearts grow. The more our hearts grow, the more room we have to soak him in and love him back. His agent to help us comprehend his Word and his Person better is the Holy Spirit.

Fittingly, the more we absorb Scripture, the more we begin to understand all the many roles of the Holy Spirit:

- He regenerates us. (John 3:5)
- He verifies we are children of God. (Romans 8:16)
- He enlightens us through God's Word. (John 14:25-26)
- He shows us who Jesus is. (John 16:12-14)
- He directs our paths. (Romans 8:14)
- He warns us. (Acts 16:6-7)
- He empowers us to overcome sin and live a godly life. (Acts 1:8)
- He comforts us in our afflictions and sorrows. (John 14:16-18)
- He intercedes in prayer for us. (Acts 8:26)

The Holy Spirit is not an it. The Holy Spirit is a who. He is the third Person of the Trinity, co-equal with God the

Father and God the Son, Jesus Christ, and not fully comprehensible to our finite minds. That's one of the reasons I chose language that is not customary to describe what he means to me in a song called "The Change in Me." As I share these lines, I'm not saying they're divine or infallible. I'm not claiming inspiration from God. But I am saying my Lord is an inspiration to me during my songwriting.

> *Your Spirit is a gentleman, standing at my hidden doors within,*
> *where you wait for me to let you in, so you can set me free.*

Sometimes lyrics wind up on my journal page and all I can think is, *Wow, that's a little more than I can pull off on my own.* We all know God does big things through little people, and this line sticks out to me. The Holy Spirit is such a gentleman. He is loving and gracious to escort us time and again to address the sin that so easily besets us. He is patient as we flounder through our selfishness. He is our chaperone through life, and he is longsuffering enough to wade into the cesspools we create and stand at the doors of our hidden rooms. God refines us through his Holy Spirit, who is jealous for his glory and the hearts of his people (Malachi 2:17-3:6).

That the Holy Spirit stands at our hidden doors and waits for us to let him in so he can set us free is a mind-blowing paradox. We're already God's children forever, but this word picture shows how we decide whether we want to let God into our prisons. He chooses us, but we decide whether we will submit to the sanctifying fire of the holiness and purity of a holy God.

Jesus says, "If anyone would come after me, let him deny himself and take up his cross and follow me. For whoever would save his life will lose it, but whoever loses his life for my sake will find it" (Matthew 16:24-25). The word "if" means it's a conditional statement. We can be God's children and still resist the leadership of his Holy Spirit. The walls we've built, the world we've created so we can have control, are cages of our own device. God's Spirit stands on the outside of our cell doors and longs to set us free.

**God alone, through the resurrection power of his Holy Spirit, can bring new life or awaken a slumbering one. Only Jesus.**

The prodigal son's spiritual awakening "when he came to himself" was prompted by God's Spirit, not by the prodigal. The prodigal didn't have the ability to wake from his slumber. God alone, through the resurrection power of his Holy Spirit, can bring new life or awaken a slumbering one. Only Jesus.

When we want to rule on the throne of our lives and make little gods of ourselves, God's Spirit constantly reaches out. He uses his Word, other people, and our circumstances to point the way back to him. When we are prodigal, he is faithful.

When I run from God and fight against his prodding, the conflict I feel comes because he's trying to set me free of bondage. When God reveals our sin to us, we think he's being hard on us and we're in big trouble. More accurately, when the Holy Spirit lights up a sin taking us in the wrong direction, he's really saying, "Let me free you from this." It's like when mom says to the toddler, "Don't touch the iron." That is a rule, yes. But she's saying, "Let me free you from being burned." We should understand all of God's commandments and precepts in this light.

God shows us the way of escape (1 Corinthians 10:13), but we often look for it much too late. For instance, I tell teenagers who are making decisions about their friends and about drinking that the way of escape isn't at the party where they're asked, "Do you want to try this?" The way of escape came earlier. It was when they were asked, "Do you want to come to the party?"

When the Holy Spirit shows us, "This is not for you. This is not the way I'm headed," and we step beyond that, we are now living in our own strength and making our own decisions. We're doing life on our own.

If Jesus is getting in your way, you're going the wrong way.

I like to use the analogy of a car's GPS to describe the Holy Spirit. Once God indwells us with his Holy Spirit at regeneration, his Spirit knows one thing to do:

"Go to the Father. Go to the Father. Go to the Father. This is where we're going. We're going to the Father."

The destination is set. We're going to the Father.

Anytime I make a wrong turn, I sense the Holy Spirit in me saying, "Recalculating."

When we veer off from what we know is biblical, the still small voice of the Holy Spirit is unrelenting because the Holy Spirit always honors the Father. He can do nothing else. He doesn't change his mind. Father, Spirit, and Son are always in perfect agreement.

*Your Spirit is a wrecking ball, tearing through my rebel walls; one by one I watch them fall, 'til you are all I see.*

Sometimes God is willing to blow up our lives to rescue us from ourselves. I have been on the wrong track but was so convinced I was living right that I became prideful about it. I'm not talking about a life of crime. I'm talking about inner walls, the kinds that hide not sinful actions but sinful motives. Outer walls have signs that say, "Stop saying bad words." Inner walls are heart issues like pride and jealousy.

I committed my life to singing for Jesus while in college. Not long afterward, I lost my voice. How's that for feeling confused? The doctor placed me on total vocal rest, and I had to walk around with a yellow note pad and pen to communicate. God took away my voice, and for a while I didn't know if I would ever sing again.

I remember wrestling with God over it. I was so confused that I didn't even understand why I was angry at him about it. I was in the middle of Bible college in Florida, I'd been married for a little over a year, and my wife worked so I could make it through college. Now I couldn't sing. My prayers weren't, "God, what are you showing me?" My prayers were, "God, you need to fix my voice. You need to come through the way I need you to come through." I was sincere. I was earnest. I prayed (demanded) hard.

He remained silent.

Then his Holy Spirit showed me that I had decided *for* God that the only way I could serve him was singing. He needed me to know that he didn't put me on this Earth to sing. He put me on this Earth to know him and make him known, and singing is only a tool toward that end. He kept me silent until he broke through my presumptions.

Right in the middle of this trial, a guy walked up to me and said, "Hey, have you ever thought about being a youth pastor?"

I shook my head and thought, *No way. I'm not being a youth pastor.*

This time, God didn't stay silent. He laughed. Thirty years later, I'm still a youth pastor. I would have missed God's great purpose for me had his Spirit not been a wrecking ball to my own ideas.

> *Your Spirit is a whispering, when all the lies are deafening; speak to the very heart of me, and fear cannot remain.*

Satan is the father of lies. God is truth. His Holy Spirit

is our indwelling antidote to the lies that besiege us at every turn. The lies say to believe what the world says about you and what you're capable of, what the world says about your past, what the world says about your family or about the bad situation you'll surely never escape. The lies are so persistent and so loud that it's hard to hear anything else.

Sometimes I wish God would come in and out-shout the lies around me, but then I remember....

It's always in the quiet moments when I hear him.

Elijah heard him in a "still small voice" or "a gentle whisper" (1 Kings 19:9-12). The point is that we are to be still and know that he is God (Psalm 46:10). I need constant reminders to stop striving and white-knuckling life so I can sense the gentle nudges of God's Spirit that, quiet as they are, drown out the loud lies.

*Your Spirit is a light ahead, calling me to the depth, and daring me to take a step, and let you lead the way.*

God's light is not only his Word but also the hope he instills in the spirit of every believer. He is our eternal flicker. His light ahead assures me that I have a hope and a future and shows me I'm not stuck. This is not the end. The best is yet to come. God's Spirit is never stagnant. He always moves, and I can trust his direction.

God's Spirit has led me into moments that I know were arranged by him, and he has led me into friendships I needed.

He has rescued me from friendships that were toxic simply by opening my eyes to a reality I had not seen. He has led me to step out of the comfortable to try a path that didn't make a lot of sense at the time.

He has led me to love people I didn't want to love. He has led me to forgive people I didn't want to forgive. He continues to illuminate the way for me to plunge deeper in my friendship with him. He was the light ahead for the Israelites in the wilderness, and he still walks me through life's deserts.

*Your Spirit is a holy flame, burning all the old away; here I am, Lord, have your way, 'til all that's left is you.*

God's Spirit constantly puts his finger on what he wants to rid from my life. I may be rude, aloof, thoughtless, sullen, or distant. I may be insensitive with a well-meaning joke. I may be prideful in digging for compliments. God's Spirit will have none of it.

I can no longer claim, "It's just my personality, so it's OK." You've heard people say stuff like, "I know I'm brash, but it's just the way I am. I'm honest."

No, they're really just being a jerk, and that's not OK.

Sometimes I just have to say, "All right, Lord, show me what's wrong. Just burn all the old way." But be ready and trust his process. He will answer that prayer, and it's not a one-day thing. It's an everyday thing.

*Your Spirit is my constant friend, you're with me 'til the very end;*
*I'll never be alone again; you're the change in me.*

At the foundation of anything a true and godly friend does for me—any warning, direction, or encouragement—I know they love me. Their love got them in the room with me to start with. It's the only reason I absorb what they say.

A godly friend is going to pray for you before she talks to you. Her love for you is part of the root system of why she's in your life.

In like manner does the Holy Spirit evidence God's love for you—whether he acts as a gentlemanly escort, a wrecking ball, a whispering, a light, or a holy flame. God does love us. He's not trying to trick us. He's not hiding from us. He's not dropping riddles to us. He's not putting a fork in the road to see what we'll do so he can taunt us with Door Number One and Door Number Two, and we're toast if we make the wrong decision. No, God's motives are ultimate, not ulterior.

He doesn't have our best interests at heart as much as he has his best interests at heart for us. Sometimes our agenda doesn't square with his, but we can rest assured that his will brings him the most glory even if it doesn't feel like it's for our best here and now.

He loves us. His love is the source of our being. He will never leave us or forsake us (Hebrews 13:5). We will never be alone. Praise God, he's the change in all of us.

## Chapter 7

# MISSHAPEN
### JEREMIAH 18:1-6

**SOMEONE CLOSE TO MELANIE** and me lost her husband. He walked out on her and left her with three children.

She was in shambles. The life she knew was in shambles. And I didn't know what to say. What happens when you're living for Jesus and your world still explodes, through no apparent fault of your own? What happens when the proverbial bad things happen to good people?

Only Jesus was enough before. What about now?

I asked this person we love, Kim, for permission to tell her story. We walked with her through devastation that was more than traumatic. It was debilitating. She always had leaned on God and on her husband, and suddenly the latter was not who she thought he was. She wondered if she could say the same about the former. Kim discovered that the primary earthly foundation on which she had rested was never really there. It was like a sinkhole opened out of nowhere, and her life was sucked out from under her. I remember sitting with her and seeing her look of disbelief and shock and sadness. It said, "I can't believe this is me. This wasn't supposed to happen to me." I felt the weight of her anguish.

"Why would God let this happen?" she said. "I don't understand. I go to church, I serve God, I try to raise my kids right. How did we get here?"

Those conversations reverberated through my mind when I sat down to write the verses of "In the Hands of the Potter." At one point Kim didn't want to pray because she didn't know where to begin. All she could think was, *God, I was trusting you, thinking that we were going in the right direction, but now I don't even know which way is up.*

I hurt with her even as I started formulating the song. After writing another section first, the opening lines poured out later:

> *I still remember when I heard you call me by name*
> *I'd follow you anywhere, knew I could trust you with anything*
> *And now sorrow beats down on me, waiting for you to come through*
> *I'm all alone with my questions, I'm dry and cracked open*
> *I thirst for you*

Kim had been waiting for God to come to the rescue, to do something, anything, and it wasn't happening. Even though she was surrounded by people who love her, she felt alone. Her closest companions were her questions. When God doesn't answer us or come through the way we want him to, it deepens the heartache. Sometimes we feel like he didn't show up. He was supposed to be our hero, and he failed us. Kim suffered through what she felt was abandonment not only from her husband but also from her heavenly Father. The moment was so raw that she despaired.

**One of the biggest misconceptions of the Christian faith is that when we get saved we suddenly have all the answers and life gets better.**

"Not only do I not know what to pray anymore, I don't know how to worship anymore," she said. "I sit in worship time and I don't know how to make it come out. I feel like I'm dry and cracked open."

Not all trials are self-inflicted. Not all of our pain is a direct result of running from God or not being in the middle of his will. One of the biggest misconceptions of the Christian faith is that when we get saved we suddenly have all the answers and life gets better. Actually, sometimes life gets worse because now we're an enemy of all of Hell.

The prodigal son brought pain upon himself, but many times we suffer heartache simply because we were born under the curse of Sin. Knowing that truth doesn't make it easier to endure. The agony is just as real, and sometimes the fact that we thought we were living for the Lord can make the trial even more confounding.

It comes down to faith, really. Do you believe that God is sovereign and loves you? Do you believe that he will forge good out of the bad? Do you believe that ultimately his purposes will be fulfilled and that he molds all things, even your pain, for his glory? Are you willing to trust him even when your suffering makes no sense at all? Do you possess that kind of faith?

It wasn't within God's will that Kim's husband left her. Even though I knew God is her hope—and deep down, so did she—I still felt her hopelessness along with her. The second verse walks through those emotions and introduces the theme of the potter's wheel.

> *My world is spinning, my life seems so out of control*
> *Nail-scarred hands tell the story of love that will never let go...*
> *of me*
> *Through the sunshine or rain, I know where my hope is found*
> *What you started in me, I know you will complete from the inside*
> *out*

I've watched a potter create a pot before. I imagined Kim in the hands of our Lord, and then I imagined myself in her place: I'm spinning so fast that my life seems out of control. I can't put my hand on any facet of my life to steady myself. I can't rest on anything right now. It seems like everything in my life is moving in different directions.

When we don't have control over our lives, we feel like

there is no control. When we're on the ultimate Potter's wheel, life can feel breathlessly out of control. We may feel cold. Dirty. Misshapen. Incomplete. But the reality is that we are in his hands.

*And as I fall apart, come flood this desert heart*
*Fall like the rain, Living Water*
*I know your way is best; Lord, help me find my rest*
*And I'll be the clay in the hands of the Potter*

As the Potter's wheel spins faster, we need the comfort of God's Holy Spirit. I need the comfort of the peace that passes all understanding that only he can give. His Spirit is our Living Water. Have you ever noticed that a potter continually dips his hands in water to reduce the friction and smooth out the bumps and lumps?

The flip side of that needed comfort of knowing that I'm in God's hands is the fact that the Potter is still at work forming me. I'm secure in his hands, but his hands are applying the pressure, and it hurts. I'm justified by Jesus. He made me right with God. But now I'm being sanctified, which means he's setting me apart and conforming me to the image of Christ. I'm working out my salvation (Philippians 2:12) and I'm surrendering one piece of myself at a time as he unveils my shortcomings and needs to me, and he's slowly forming me to look more like Jesus.

All believers are predestined to be conformed to the image of Christ (Romans 8:29). He never stops spiritually forming us, always with different intensities and pressures, and the pain and pressure can seem unbearable. But he spins away at the wheel, adding substance to our base and smoothing out this bump and sharpening that ridge. And the wheel spins faster and the hand feels heavier....

Matthew 8:23-27 chronicles a scene that strikes me as foreign and familiar at the same time. Jesus is asleep in a boat that is taking on water. The disciples wake him by crying, "Save us, Lord. We're perishing." I can't imagine being in a storm on the sea, especially in a small vessel. But these are seasoned fishermen, and the storm is bad enough that they fear for their lives.

**When we come to the end of our control, it's a scary place to live.**

The disciples trust him with so many areas of their lives. They realize he can feed people. He can heal people. He can even raise the dead. They've witnessed these miracles. But this is different. This is the sea. This storm is not normal. If anyone knows how abnormal it is, these fishermen do. Here is an area where Jesus doesn't have their trust yet—they don't trust him with their world. They trust God with everybody else's world. They trust him with other people's diseases and other people's hunger and other people's demon possession. But this is their ocean, their world they come from, and when they're no longer in control they think surely they're going to die. They shake him awake with the abrupt words, "Lord, do you even care?"

As God is forming us into the image of his Son, sooner or later he's going to hit a place that we don't realize we're still holding onto for ourselves. Or maybe it's an area in which we're still making things work on our own and haven't had to trust him yet. When we come to the end of our control, it's a scary place to live. We don't have our footing and we feel like we're spinning. We have to remind ourselves that it's only a feeling, but we experience it deeply nonetheless.

Sometimes it's so deep that it hurts to breathe. And so it was with Kim. She suffered.

Kim trusted God with her kids. She trusted God with the finances. She trusted God with her health. But her husband? He was just supposed to be there. He had been there for years and years. And then one day he wasn't, and essentially every earthly thing she knew changed.

I wrote the bridge to this song before I wrote anything else. I was sitting in the back of the tour bus after talking with Kim on the phone. I opened my journal and wrote, "When my world is breaking me, your love is shaping me, and the enemy is scared of what you're making me." The song is sourced from the truth that what the enemy would mean for bad, God will work for good. Not only will he heal me, but he also will make me into something new through my trial. He may not restore what I had, but he will conform me into Christ's image even more, and some day he will bring good out of my struggles— even if the only good was that somehow he was glorified. We should all pray for such a contented faith.

Before giving Jeremiah a prophecy about Israel, God told him to go watch a potter:

"So I went down to the potter's house, and there he was working at his wheel. And the vessel he was making of clay was spoiled in the potter's hand, and he reworked it into another vessel, as it seemed good to the potter to do" (Jeremiah 18:3-4).

Only one Potter has the power to mold us when we're spiritually misshapen. Only Jesus. When life is breaking us down, God is building us up, and even when dark things are coming to us, light is coming from him. All followers of Christ can look back to difficult times in which only now do we realize we were in the Potter's hands and he was forming us.

My biggest Potter's Hands moment was when I built my life around a girl at age 19 and the girl went away. Only then did I realize I needed to know him and draw from him. In one of the darkest times of my life, God formed in me what ended up being my calling to ministry, my gifts, and my life's purpose.

So strongly did God spin me on his wheel that it didn't matter that I had dyslexia and ADD. It didn't matter that I was petrified of standing in front of people and trying to lead anything. God spun that fear into dependence on him. He spun that fear into a confidence that didn't have to be in myself. Suddenly the confidence was in him.

Time after time, I have endured seasons in which I felt my life was totally out of control and thought, *God, there's no way this is going to work.* The Potter's wheel felt like it was going to wobble off its base in my battle with kidney cancer a few years ago. I lost a kidney and came up with a song called "O My Soul" during that ordeal. In each trial God has stepped into the moment and showed me something new about him and conformed me a little more into the likeness of Christ.

My Potter's Hands moments have never come in peaceful times. They've always surfaced in difficult, painful times in which I had no choice but to look up. I had no choice but to realize he would have to move. Otherwise, nothing positive or fruitful was conceivable. I've learned that when we finally stop trying to form ourselves and handcraft our solutions and manipulate our situations and realize there's no way that even Plans B, C, or D will work, only then do we let go and trust the Potter to rework us into whatever vessel he chooses. We finally rest in the Potter's hands. Admittedly, it's a scary thought. It doesn't mean we're resting into a peaceful moment. No, we're resting into a painful moment in which we trust that God is going to work.

When God's Word tells us to rest, there's a reason. It means an anxious moment is happening and we're not resting. It doesn't mean we'll now enjoy soft music, a softer pillow, and a big sigh. It just means that we're going to have to let go and trust the Potter to form us as he desires.

I wish I could give you a happily-ever-after ending to Kim's story. Her husband hasn't come back. Her hope is still in God, but the wheel is still spinning fast. I keep reminding her that what feels like constant pressure is proof of the presence of his hands. She may feel misshapen, but she's in his grip. She's still the clay in the hands of the Potter.

## Chapter 8

Listen: Start Right Here

# DISTANCE
## 2 CHRONICLES 7:14; LUKE 15:25-32

**WE WANT CHANGE.**

We want our country to change. We want our government leaders to change. We want our bosses to change. We want our jobs to change. We want our homes to change. We want our spouses to change. We want our kids to change. We even want our churches to change. We want everything to change.

Everything, that is, except us.

We don't need to change. We're just fine. If everybody could just be more like us....

The song "Start Right Here" is my candid response to what I see happening in the Church today. It is meant not as criticism but as a loving reminder from an accountability partner. It is no coincidence that the first two sections of the first verse and the chorus all begin with the words, "We want...." That pretty much sums up the attitude of Americans today.

I'm afraid it has permeated Christ's Church.

Sometimes it seems like we forget that God's grace and mercy to us is the same grace and mercy he extends to others. It's like we forget how his Holy Spirit awakened us, saved us out of the pigpen, and, many times thereafter, restored us from our wayward choices.

While on tour, I travel to large churches throughout America. I see a lot of ministries and hear a lot of opinions, and I fear our younger generation of believers is being groomed more as consumers than disciples. I often see people shopping for the right churches and saying things like, "We're going to go to the church across town because the worship is more free." Or, "I'm going to go find a church that's more friendly and welcoming." Or, "I'm going to find a church that has a better (fill in the blank) ministry."

In all of that chatter, what I hear is, "Let's find a church that we need" instead of, "Let's become the church that everybody else needs." While more people search out churches that have all they want, fewer people want to make a church what it's supposed to be. Such motives are wrong and dangerous.

People will flock 45 minutes to visit a big contemporary church because the worship is so free, but the big church is playing the same songs as the church they just left. Somehow it feels freer at the popular church. I hear people say, "Everyone's hands are in the air and everyone's singing loudly."

My response?

"Well, why aren't you doing that where you are?"

It's like they don't realize they've moved to a room full of strangers, so it's easier to feel free. It's not freer. It's more disconnected. They don't know the people in the room, so they don't care what anyone thinks.

If we were a little more bold in our original church, we could set an atmosphere where people could worship and raise hands and sing as loudly as they want right where they are. But we want permission from a room that will break the ice for us. We want to go find a church instead of *being* the Church. We must start being the Church God intended. It's got to start somewhere. It's got to start right here, Church. It's got to start with each individual believer.

> **We must start being the Church God intended. It's got to start somewhere.**

Before my mailbox is overrun with letters of outrage, I'll share with you my heart behind the stiff lyrics about coffee in the lobby, worship on the screen, and rock star preachers. It's all a reminder that we're supposed to be there for the church and not the other way around. We shouldn't walk into a building full of fellow believers with the attitude of an audience ready to watch another episode of church this week. We should never walk in the doors ready to see what this place has to offer us rather than what we bring to everyone else.

We've become so consumer-minded that we're in danger of trying to create a more comfortable experience in a building. Meanwhile, we don't give nearly as much thought to what we're doing outside that building to love on the world.

The strange phenomenon of the rock star preacher is not modern. In 1 Corinthians 1:10-17, Paul corrects believers in Corinth torn over whom to follow. Some people gravitate to Paul, others to Apollos or Peter. Paul scolds them for creating division in the church and later explains why they're infatuated with the preacher and not the Lord who's being preached.

"I fed you with milk, not solid food, for you were not ready for it. And even now you are not yet ready, for you are still of the flesh. For while there is jealousy and strife among you, are you not of the flesh and behaving only in a human way? For when one says, 'I follow Paul,' and another, 'I follow Apollos,' are you not being merely human" (1 Corinthians 3:2–4)?

The Corinthians elevated personalities and convinced themselves that they only learned well from certain teachers. Sound familiar?

As helpful as it is to soak in good teaching from a nationally known preacher—and I use and love many such resources—that's not church. A great worship concert is terrific. The feelings, the emotions, and the messages the Holy Spirit speaks to us in those environments are wonderful, but that's not church. Driving 45 minutes away to a building once a week and then saying goodbye to those people until the next week is not church.

We'll stare at a pastor from 600 miles away on a screen as he gets all up in our business because we know we can turn him off anytime we want. But to allow a real, live pastor stand in front of us and step into our lives? That's Church.

Caveat: I know plenty of people who, because of work schedules and life situations, must watch a telecast or webcast of worship services. Maybe they're sick, injured, or elderly. Maybe they're a caregiver. It's perfectly understandable and I applaud their tuning into the service. But that in itself is not church. Church includes relationship, accountability, and community. That's why it's called the Body of Christ. I fear we've retreated from letting the Church into the core of our worlds. We've found a way to keep it at a distance.

We also keep our missions at a distance. It's a lot easier to support something on the other end of the planet, because we give once and it's done. We take some supplies to the church, and it's over. As great as that is, I have to ask myself, "Of course I need to send supplies around the world. Of course I need to give toward this missions offering. Of course I do. But somewhere along the way, have I accidentally trained myself to think that "missions" is somewhere else and not here?"

Do my hands ever get dirty in missions? What about my community? What about my city or neighborhood? What can I do here *also*? Not instead of, but also. What can I do to cut the distance between my faith and my life?

What's happening right here, right now, in my faith life? In my friendships? At my work? Is it real and practical? Or is everything about my faith kept at a distance? We want to see people's hearts set free and we want to see tyrants kneel. We want to see the walls fall down and the land be healed. But if we want to see a change in the world out there, it's got to start right here.

While we drift further away from what Church is supposed to be, it seems we're getting more involved in what we think the world is supposed to be.

We fire out opinions and convictions in tweets and posts, and we take a stand on everything that's somewhere else. It's amazing how many of us have an opinion on a major issue until that issue shows up in our family. It's so much easier to throw a rock at somebody far away. We take our stands on things that don't cost us. When it does not cost us to take a stand on something, maybe we don't need to say what we're about to say. Maybe that's for someone else to take a stand on— someone who is actually in the trenches in that particular problem or heartache.

> **It's so much easier to throw a rock at somebody far away. We take our stands on things that don't cost us.**

I've learned the hard way that when we throw our words, we rarely hit the people we're aiming at; we almost always hit someone else. We feel like we're close to a lot of the controversial topics of our day just because they're on a social media app on our phones. Biblical Christianity is personal, not impersonal. It's an invitation, not a condemnation.

We want politicians to take care of everything. We want our pet causes at the forefront. We want all the right laws passed. I'm all for voting our scripturally informed conscience, but no president is going to save our country. No president is going to save our families. He or she does not exist. One Person will.

Only Jesus.

We want laws to take care of all the bad stuff for us. The tyrants that we want to kneel and the walls that we want to see fall down? We can't legislate that. But 2 Chronicles 7:14 says, "If my people who are called by my name humble themselves, and pray and seek my face and turn from their wicked ways, then I will hear from heaven and will forgive their sin and heal their land."

That's an if-then statement. There's not even a way to mess up that verse. There's no way to read it wrong. It starts with the Church. In our heart of hearts, we really do want the walls that divide us to fall down and the land to be healed, but when we examine where the Church is headed, it's not going anywhere near the direction of 2 Chronicles 7:14.

The reason, ironically enough, can be found in yet another person in the story of the prodigal son.

***

We've seen the prodigal's wanton sin and his awakening. We've seen the Holy Spirit's role in his awakening and renewal. We've seen how love moved first in the father's response to his lost son's desperate need. Now we get to see the person a lot of Christians are in this story. Many of us are the prodigal's elder brother.

Both the prodigal son and the elder brother wanted the stuff that went along with their father, but they didn't want their father. One grieved his father by being a sinful rebel. The other grieved his father with his righteousness—his own righteousness.

The elder brother turned his nose and puffed his chest at his father's response to his wayward brother. He didn't run off like his brother, but his soul was just as dead. This is the brother who stayed home. He did what he was supposed to do. He did his chores. He worked hard. He led. He was there for his dad. He gave blood, sweat, and tears his whole life, but along with it came a sense of self-righteousness and entitlement. He didn't value his place in the family as the son of a loving and benevolent father. Instead, he found his worth in what he did and didn't do.

His attitude screamed, "I'm working hard. I'm serving. I'm here every time I'm needed. I don't run off and waste my life. I don't party. I don't hang around with bad characters. I'm better than that little brat." Instead of grasping the fact that his father loved and accepted him as a dear son, he believed he made himself a worthy son by his conduct.

The elder brother compared himself to his younger brother and figured he was better. Instead of celebrating his younger brother's homecoming, he resented his return. Instead of empathizing with a loved one who caved to the flesh, he heralded his own perceived glory. Instead of walking a mile in someone else's shoes, he wouldn't even walk across the yard to hug his rescued brother.

Sometimes we can get in the bubble of church world and look at everyone else through behavior glasses. Or we see others through our affinities and groups and likes and personal experiences. Instead of looking at them through Jesus' eyes, we look through our own filters, and, when we see people who don't live like we do, we get mad at them. I call it "sinvy"—short for *sin envy*. We actually resent them for getting the pleasure of doing what lost people do.

> **Instead of walking a mile in someone else's shoes, he wouldn't even walk across the yard to hug his rescued brother.**

It's awful when you're trying to lose weight and you eat with a skinny person who goes to the all-you-can-eat buffet. You can't enjoy your little serving for thinking, *Why am I working so hard and I'm still a blimp, and yet this little rail can inhale anything he wants?*

We're good at hiding it, but sometimes we grow bitter when the world gets to scratch the itches that our flesh longs to get scratched. Something rises up in us because depriving the flesh is hard. It's hard to say no to the world. It's hard to rationalize other people's behavior.

*I want to live a clean life, but look at how these people who call themselves members of our church family live. They're here every Sunday after doing whatever they want on Saturday night. Their hands are in the air during worship, and yet they were probably falling off the curb at the club last night.*

We compare ourselves to others to make ourselves feel better. We see their shortcomings, and the elder brother in us rolls his eyes.

When trouble hits and we suffer, it's easy to grow angry as we compare ourselves to others who seem to float through life. We look at them like the elder brother looked at the prodigal. We feel that since we live right, we should be blessed in ways that benefit us right here and right now. This is self-centered and shortsighted.

First, we never know what's going on in other people's lives, which makes comparison such a devil's lie. We never know how badly others are struggling—no matter how shiny their packaging. Secondly, the bottom line is that it doesn't matter what we want. It matters what God wants. And you know what God wants?

Change.

## Chapter 9

Listen: The Bridge

# BRIDGE BUILDERS
## JOHN 13:35; PHILIPPIANS 1:27-30

**ONE OF MY MOST ANTICIPATED** moments in high school was a beach trip with two friends. It was the first time we got to go to the beach by ourselves. We thought we were living on the edge, man. Three dudes, a halfway cool car, and 175 miles of "bro time" while jazzed on the kind of adrenaline that only untethered youth can produce.

My friend Rex was just starting to live for Jesus. He was the first friend I had who decided that God was going to be the center of his life. I'd never seen anyone my age truly live for Jesus outside of church.

As we traveled south and listened to the radio, Rex grew convicted of our choice of radio stations.

"Guys, maybe we shouldn't listen to this," he said. "Listen to this for me."

He popped in a cassette tape of a Christian band. I thought, *All right. That's cool…I guess. I'm a Christian. I get it.*

Our friend Doug stayed silent. At the time it didn't occur to me that he wasn't a believer. I hadn't grown enough to know how to gauge someone's spiritual condition. Rex, on the other hand, didn't leave much room for guessing. When we trashed somebody, he would interrupt and say, "Maybe we shouldn't talk about him like that." When the speech got a little coarse, he would say, "Guys, let's watch our language." Those little moments stood out in our crowd. I knew Rex was right, but it also struck me as awkward and weird.

When we stopped at a store on the way to the beach, Rex went inside while Doug and I waited in the car.

"You know," Doug said, "I like Rex and all, but he's just...he's just not like us."

"What do you mean?" I said.

"I don't know, man. I just don't know about all this Jesus stuff. I mean, he's just not like us."

I was stunned.

"What do you mean 'us'?" I said. "I'm a Christian too."

"Oh," Doug said. "OK...well...that's cool."

He didn't know!

One of my best friends had no clue I was a believer. I thought it was clear who I was. I wasn't a drinker. I didn't party. I didn't smoke. I didn't do anything considered bad or rebellious. Still, I didn't produce any evidence that I belonged to Christ just as much as Rex did. I had yet to hear the old saying, "If loving God were a crime, would there be enough evidence to convict you?"

What did convict me was my exchange with Doug. It alarmed me that nothing in me pointed to Jesus. I was about 18. It would be another year before the Lord awakened me after the breakup with my girlfriend.

\*\*\*

I LEARNED ANOTHER VALUABLE lesson when I was a teenager—one that helped me when I became a youth pastor. I learned it's good to invite guest speakers to teach your students from time to time. When I was a kid, we seldom had guest speakers at our small church. Our youth pastor taught us. Every. Single. Week. I now know it's good to have a guest speaker come in even if he says the exact same thing I say every week, because sometimes the kids hear it for the first time.

I usually ask a guest speaker to lead our sessions during summer camp, and invariably several students approach me throughout the week. The conversations are always similar.

"Mark! This speaker this week has changed my life! He said that we should read our Bible EVERY DAY! Can you believe this? I'm so stoked!"

"That's really cool, Biff. I'm really glad we brought in this guy to tell you that. By the way, what is this Bible of which you speak? I've never heard of it."

Strange phenomenon, I know, but it also happened to me when I was a kid. A guest speaker detailed the medical aspects of what happened to Jesus on the Cross. I was riveted. I hadn't heard that when someone hangs from a cross, it's not the excruciation from the nails that kills him—it's suffocation. It's a slow, miserable death as your body weakens while fluid builds in your lungs and around your heart, and you slowly stop breathing. When you hang in such a position, it puts pressure on your lungs, and the only way to breathe is to use your legs to push up on the nail through your feet, increasing the agony. This was new information for me long before Mel Gibson made his movie, *The Passion of the Christ* or Lee Strobel wrote, *A Case for Christ*.

Then the speaker said something I can still quote.

"There are people in this world I would die for. My family? I would die for them in a heartbeat if the choice was between one of them dying or my dying. There are people I love and for whom I would sacrifice myself," he said. "And if someone were to come in here tonight and take this group hostage and say, 'The only way we're going to let these kids out of here alive is if we take you instead,' you know what? I love God. I know I'm saved. I've lived a good life. I might even do that. There are a lot of people for whom I would die."

Then he paused to look around the room and let the moment build.

"But there isn't anybody I would give my son for."

I don't think anyone moved or even blinked.

"If someone were to come in here and take us hostage and tell me that they'll let you hostage kids free if I'll give them my son, I'm sorry, but you guys would be toast."

I sat there with my mouth half open. I had never considered the depth of Christ's sacrifice in such terms, and it was like God's love got a little bigger for me that day. I had a little better understanding of how much it cost God for me to get to him. It cost him his Son.

I remember another time in high school when a guy sang a solo in church with a chorus that says, *"You're the only Jesus some will ever see. You're the only book of life some will ever read."*

It was a song by the Imperials, and it really got me. I had never heard of Contemporary Christian music. I thought the only Christian music was hymns. But when he sang that lyric, it stirred me that not everybody goes to church. Not everybody has a Bible. Not everybody hears all the sermons I hear. The only gospel they may ever get is whatever I bring them.

> **I had a little better understanding of how much it cost God for me to get to him. It cost him his Son.**

All of these moments were formative for me. I saw how much it cost God for Jesus to be the bridge to God for me, and I realized that the way I live either builds a bridge to Jesus or holds up a road sign that says, "Bridge Is Out," and they want nothing to do with the Lord because of what they see in me.

If we can have the humility to admit that we are sinners

that God had to awaken through his Holy Spirit, then God will use that same humility to make us nobodies content to be bridge builders for other souls running away from God and in desperate need of only Jesus.

***

IN THOSE SAME TEEN YEARS, several people explained what Jesus did for me by using a word picture I still remember.

They described two cliffs with a giant canyon in the middle and God on one side of the canyon and me on the other. Sin had caused that canyon—not my personal sins but the power and presence of Sin—our fallen state—that entered mankind in the Garden of Eden. That Sin, with a capital S, is why I commit personal sins. They explained that God is love but God also is just. He loves me for who he made me, but I'm fallen. God is holy and cannot have fellowship with darkness, so that canyon separates me from him. The word picture always included a cross spanning the canyon to bridge the divide between God and me.

Christ's Cross proved that he came to build a bridge to God for us. Love moved first. I've never had a problem understanding that Jesus built the bridge to God for us. However, it took a while for me to realize that we believers are the bridge that leads people to Jesus.

As I look back on my formative years, I'm grateful at how often God sent people to build a bridge to Jesus for me.

At first, they seemed like professional Christians, people who were just doing what they were supposed to do at church. After God awakened me, I slowly realized Luke Finkelstein was the real deal. He ran a pawn shop, and he wasn't exactly a cool dude. He was probably in his late 20's and heavy set with a short haircut. He usually wore Sansabelt slacks, the pants with the built-in belt that a lot of middle-aged men wore. He didn't impact me with the way he looked, however. He

> **Christ's Cross proved that he came to build a bridge to God for us.**

impacted me with how he lived. He was one of the first Christians I noticed who applied Scripture to daily life in a way that made sense to me.

"Somebody stole from my shop this week," he said one time. "I'm really praying about it, that God's going to help me forgive this guy and do the right thing."

All of us kids were thinking, *Justice, man. Put him away.*

Yet Luke actually was praying about his response. Just the fact that he involved his faith as he tried to figure out how to handle a difficult experience was different for me.

I started seeing that Debbie McGregor's worship was not just about performing songs. She led the church to worship because she truly worshipped. I could tell her only audience was God. I started noticing Mr. Short, our college and career class leader, would make comments that had weight. They weren't out of the lesson book but were steeped in the truth of Scripture and borne out in his life.

I started keying in to the truth that God had placed people in my life to lead me to more than just church. They were leading me to Jesus. It began to dawn on me that I needed to do the same for other people too. Then I started reading the Bible for myself and seeing that some people's whole lives were dedicated to building a bridge to Jesus by what they said, what they did, and how they handled things.

For instance, in Philippians 1:12-18, the Apostle Paul is in one of the darkest times of his life and yet tells us all from whom our joy should come. It's the most upbeat, positive book in the New Testament, and Paul is in a dungeon when he writes it.

"It's turned out to be great that I'm here in prison," he says.

What kind of madness is that?

Paul is content that God is using his unjust imprisonment to show the whole palace guard, people who are lost and yet in charge of him, that he is there because of his belief in Jesus. The guards and the prisoners know he's weathering this storm for Jesus. He made it clear he wasn't a victim but a victor.

How I handle difficulties and storms in my life can build a bridge to Jesus. It can show people around me that he's real and is everything he said he is, and that God is good even though my day may be bad. We can be that bridge-builder, or we can be a roadblock that says, "All is lost. That was all cool for Sunday, but it ain't working in my life."

Later, in verses 27-28, Paul encourages us to live a life worthy of the gospel. Obviously he's not saying we can live a life worthy of God's love; no one is worthy of a righteous God's perfect love. Instead, he tells us to live a life worthy of the *gospel*. I should live in such a way that it wouldn't seem out of place if I were to point to Jesus—wherever I am, and whomever I'm with. Some moments might seem random. Like, "Hey, the pass the ketchup. Did you know all men have sinned and fallen short of God's glory?" But in my friend-ships, if I were to say to them that I'm a believer, they should be able look at me and say, "Of course you are."

All around me, God sent my personal cloud of wit-nesses who decided their lives were going to be a bridge to Jesus in some way. They were going to serve, they were going to give, they were going to go on mission trips, they were going to pour into kids, they were going to do anything they could do to build a bridge for someone who didn't know God. Whatever it was, they were willing to do it. I was only a young adult, but I realized I needed to be that for other people.

Slowly but surely, my heart fixated on the truths that Jesus built a bridge to God and I'm supposed to build a bridge to Jesus for others. When people looked at me, I wanted them to see only one person. Not me. Only Jesus.

## Chapter 10

# THREE MINUTES OF COURAGE
## JOHN 13:35; PHILIPPIANS 1:27-30

**ONE DAY AS WE DROVE** home from bowling, I sat in the passenger seat of my friend Garner's car and knew it was time for one awkward moment. My chest pounded as I turned to him.

"Garner, man, you know I go to church, and you know I'm a Christian, right?"

"Yeaaahhhh?" he said.

Think comedian Jim Gaffigan. Garner was brilliant and a little dry and gruff, and he sort of grunted out the word in the form of a question. He was a deep thinker, which made me want to talk to him about Jesus even less because I knew he was going to have some crazy question I couldn't answer. He was a smart guy with a natural sarcasm about him.

I paused.

"Are you about to start talking to me about Jesus?" he said.

He actually said that.

I paused again and thought, *OK, here we go.*

"Man, all I know is that Christ has changed my life, I love you, and I want you to be in Heaven with me one day."

That's all I knew to say to broach the subject.

This time, he was the one who paused.

"I know," he said. "I know you do. I understand."

That's all I needed to hear. I thought, *I'm just going to go for it. We're out here now.*

"I've read these verses," I said, and then quoted all five verses: Romans 3:23; 6:23; 5:8; 10:9-10; and 10:13.

"To be a believer, you have to believe the truth in those verses with all your heart and trust God to save you, and you have to turn from your sins and place all your faith in him."

I felt a massive relief just getting through the verses, but I had no idea how he would respond. Would he pull over to the side of the road and fall to his knees? Would he try to debate me? Would he kick me out of his car?

Garner kept his eyes straight ahead and offered a response I never would've guessed.

"I appreciate that," he said. "Thanks."

I laugh about it now, but at the moment I thought, *Well, that was it. I've managed to blow my one shot. He's never going to turn to the Lord because I'm not a good enough Christian. I'm not a smart enough Christian. I've got nothing.*

He dropped me off at home, and I went inside a little depressed and muttering to myself.

*Well, that was it. I didn't do it right.*

At the same time, I felt the deep satisfaction of someone who at least tried to do what he is supposed to do.

\*\*\*

AS A YOUNG BELIEVER, I came to understand that I had a personal relationship with Jesus and he didn't live at church. Our church building wasn't the only place I was supposed to meet with him.

I got saved when I was nine, and at first I thought church was something we did on Sunday and Wednesday. We did baseball on Tuesday and Thursday. Games were on Saturday. I had different sets of friends at school, at baseball, and then at church, which seemed like just one more world we visited. I was still a child, and yet it was amazing how I compartmentalized my world.

In my teen years, I heard people at church say God is supposed to reign over all my life. So I would ask a friend from baseball to come to church with me, or I'd have a friend from school come to a youth event.

Slowly, Jesus began to bleed into my other worlds. I would be with a friend who was going through a tough time, and I would think, *God can really help him.* That was about the extent of my theology at first. I had heard we need to tell people about Jesus, but I just sort of packed it away with all the other little sermons I heard. As I moved toward young adulthood, the Holy Spirit started nudging me toward people in my world who weren't saved. I had realizations like, "Man, I don't think David is a believer. What does that mean for him? What does it mean for me?"

All I knew to think at first was he's going to Hell and not Heaven. As I grew older and matured spiritually, I noticed things going on in my friends' families that seemed scary and unknown. I knew I should pray about it, but I didn't know how. I didn't know what to say or how to tell them about God. But I came to a greater realization that a whole world out there doesn't know Jesus, and some of them are my friends and people I love. And how can you love somebody and not tell your friend about Jesus if he really is who you say he is?

That's when I came to a startling conclusion: All the Sunday School teachers were right. All the preachers were right. All the Scripture verses were right. We're actually supposed to share the gospel with people.

I remember learning the five verses of the Romans Road in Royal Ambassadors, the ministry that equipped young people with the gospel. But then came the hard part. How in the world would I work the gospel into the kickball game in my neighborhood? There's no easy bridge to build there. I didn't see a way to get from a game to the gospel. We're playing "Tackle the Man With the Ball" in the front yard, and how do you get from there to, "Let me tell you about Jesus?" I never could find the connection on how to do that. The older I got, the more I understood that the only connection that mattered was the relationships themselves. If I cared about my friends, I wouldn't care about one awkward moment.

I can't tell you how many times I've heard the same excuse from people reluctant to share the gospel with loved ones because, "I don't want to ruin our friendship."

"What you're basically saying," I always answer, "Is you love your friendship more than you love your friend."

Before I fully understood the need to share the gospel with people like Garner, I would've used the same excuse. The gospel says I must be ready to put the friendship on the line to tell my friend the truth. That is true love. I need to love them that much because I made it into their world. No preacher is going to crack this circle. It's just a few friends and me. It's four people on my team and me. It's three people on my job project and me. It's just us. The only missionary God has assigned to this circle is me.

> **The gospel says I must be ready to put the friendship on the line to tell my friend the truth. That is true love.**

If you truly love her, your friend is worth one awkward moment. And the dread of that one awkward moment is exactly what holds us back:

*I don't know what to say. How do I start? When do I try? What if she has a question I can't answer? What if she's mad at God? Maybe God did something in her life she didn't like, and I don't know what to do with that.*

We feel the dilemma of fearing for our loved one's eternity but also fearing we're going to push her away. If we could muster three minutes of courage, maybe the icebreaker would sound something like this:

"Hey, I need to tell you something. I need to tell you that I love you. I need to tell you that I've trusted God to save me. I'm still messing up and I still fall down, but he's with me anyway. And I know that if he can save me, he can save you, and I'd love to tell you more about my relationship with him and how you can have a relationship with him. I just want you to know the truth. You've got me as a friend and I've got your back and I'm praying for you."

Through telling your story and showing your scars, you've earned the right through your relationship to speak truth to your friend. Love earns the right to speak truth. But truth proves that you really love. To love someone and never tell her the truth is to never really love her.

Could this be the day that you come to the rescue? She's desperate for the light but she's never going to ask you. It's on you to offer one word or one hand and push through that one awkward moment. Here are a few reminders to help make room for it:

### Make time to listen.

Listen for ways to pray for your friend. When you hear her venting about family drama, guess what? You're going to pray for her now. Every time you pray, you're going to pray for your friend's situation. You hear your friend talking about getting cut from the team or worried about a job or a medical diagnosis, and now you have an icebreaker. You promise to pray for her, and the next time you're with her all you have to say is, "Hey, how's it going with what you told me? I've been praying for you."

You know what you just did? You just brought Jesus into your friendship and built a bridge to him. You just told your friend that you are calling out her name to God when she's not around. Does it mean you will automatically get to share the gospel in that moment? Probably not. She will hear your response and say thanks. But she's never going to forget what you just said. You're the friend who prays for her.

At other times, you can use conversation to steer her thoughts toward God. Seize the opportunity when your friend compliments you. Respond, "Thank you. I've been praying about that, and I really needed that." Take the opportunity to point to the Lord in little moments. You're putting God on the radar, and you'll find it amazing how often the subject surfaces again later, and sometimes your friend is willing to bring up another issue and say, "Hey, can you pray for me about this too?"

Your friend will know you truly love her when you're willing to pray for her. It's bigger than "We both like movies." It's a 3D friendship, which is deeper than getting along with each other, liking the same clothes, and laughing at the same jokes. Rather, it's a spiritual third level to a friendship.

**Make war on the floor.**

If you promise to pray for your friend, then make sure to pray for her. This is not a passing "Hey, I'll pray for you" statement. No, this means that you really are praying for your friend. And the more you pray for her, the more God is going to put her on your heart.

Earnest prayer changes my perspective of my friend even more, and suddenly I see the gravity of her living without Jesus, with no spiritual compass and no light in her world. It breaks your heart for your friend even more, so your praying for her comes before you ever say anything else or mention the gospel.

I'll go ahead and put this out there: If you haven't prayed for your friend, don't say anything to her. Stay out of her way, because all you're going to do is give her some bad advice just like everybody else. Christians can give terrible counsel too. If you're not praying for your friend, just skip to the next chapter. But if you'll start listening to her and praying for her, then you're ready for the next step.

**Make sure to follow through.**

Here's part of your prayer for your friend:

"Lord, if you give me the moment, if you give me the chance, I'll push through it. If you give me a chance to share the gospel with my friend, I'll do it."

Be prepared. If you pray that prayer, God is going to answer it 100 percent of the time, but only if you mean it.

Don't pray it if you don't mean it. But if you mean it, one awkward moment will happen sooner than you think, and it won't be nearly as awkward as you fear.

\*\*\*

I WAS A SENIOR IN HIGH SCHOOL the first time I realized that Garner didn't know Jesus. I thought I was the only person in his world who did. I sensed even more pressure because we were about to graduate. I realized I had to tell Garner about Jesus, and it scared me to death. I didn't know how to begin. I knew all the verses, but like most believers, I was trained well beyond my obedience. Most of us already have all the knowledge we could ever need.

I'm 49 now, and I still remember thinking, *I'm scared, I'm nervous, but I love Garner more than I'm scared.* I plunged headlong into my awkward moment.

Let me show you how God works. About five years ago, Garner reached out to me.

"Man, I want you to know I've made some rough decisions in my life," he said. "Some things happened."

He talked about a marriage that didn't last. He shared a few other problems. He worked in law enforcement and had tried a lot of different things in life, but he never could get out of his head that I, as a scared teenager, told him about Jesus.

"It just always stayed with me," he said. "I want you to know that I've trusted Jesus and I'm a believer and I'm in a church here in my city, and I've got my kids in church. I really appreciate what you did for me."

I had gone decades thinking that my first time sharing the gospel was one of the biggest failures in my Christian life. I always felt a little embarrassed even thinking about it. Instead, through those intervening years, God slowly germinated the truth I shared to help bring Garner to him.

The goal for the believer is not to save somebody. We can't do that. The goal for the believer is to share the truth in love. That's all we can do.

One word, one hand—tell me, is that too high a price? One awkward moment could be the one that saves a life.

## Chapter 11

Listen: One More Song For You

# Hold My Hand
## Matthew 28:18-20; Philippians 1:19-26

**I didn't know I was a songwriter** when I started writing songs. To me, it was just an act of worship as I drove down the road toward school.

I had a 45-minute drive, one way, to Bible college. Then, as now, my favorite writing lab is behind the wheel of a car. I didn't call it songwriting at first because I didn't intend to do anything more with my little creations other than lift them up to the Lord. The lyrics and melodies that slowly emerged were the natural outpouring of what I learned as I dug into God's Word more and more. Then, as now, the more I fed on Scripture, the more truth worked its way out of me.

I found myself making up songs about trials I was dealing with, and I didn't even realize I was doing it. When I did realize it, I just figured everybody did the same thing. I had no idea it would become one of my vocations, and it would be a long time until I ever shared a note with anyone other than God.

The first song I ever wrote was called "Hold My Hand," and it was a prayer about a tough job situation. It's probably one of the worst songs ever written, right up there with "Always and Forever" in *Napoleon Dynamite*. But I didn't write it for anybody else. I wrote it for me:

> *Lord, it's been a bad day today*
> *My job is so hard; my boss is so mean*
> *Sometimes I don't know what he wants from me*
> *Lord, just living from day to day*
> *It takes a lot of strength that I don't have*
>
> *Hold my hand—over mountains, Lord*
> *Hold my hand—through the valleys*
> *When I feel so all alone*
> *Hold my hand*
> *When I feel that I can't go on*
> *There's a peace in your eyes*
> *Hold my hand*

Yes, it was that bad, but I would weep as I sang the chorus because it was from the bottom of my heart. Finding the courage to share those lyrics publicly reminds me of a joke from Christian comedian Tim Hawkins, describing songwriters who say that God "gave" them a song.

"Sometimes," Tim said, "I just want to tell them, 'Maybe you should give it back.'"

While I know he's joking, I do think God sometimes lets us get our feelings out in a song that may not be for the whole world to hear. "Hold My Hand" was one of them.

About the same time I began tinkering with songs, I also started teaching teenagers in youth group. I was scared to death to stand before a crowd and teach, so I sang songs from artists like Steven Curtis Chapman. I showed my students the lyrics and then the Scripture verses that the lyrics came from, and that's how I would teach the lesson.

One day I decided it was time to use one of my own songs, called "Nothing's Too Big For My Jesus." All I had was the chorus, and it was the first time I ever sang one of my songs out loud for a group.

> *There's nothing too big for my Jesus*
> *No mountain too high, no valley too low*
> *There's no sin too dark for my Jesus*
> *For the blood he shed*
> *Can wash you white as snow*

I would play it on my little keyboard and we would sing it in our prayer times together. Really, it was just another version of "Hold My Hand" but with a little more growth.

The first full song I ever completed was "How Will They Know?" It was about sharing the Gospel. As much as I had struggled in math, I started putting my version of two and two together. God had gifted me to sing and come up with lyrical ideas. The more I learned from Scripture, and the more I worked on my songs, the better they got. What God was teaching me at that time became what I taught my students through songs, which then could be shared and sung with people. Without teaching students, I don't know that I would've ever completed anything more than a few praise ditties to hum in the car.

From that point on, the more I taught and poured into students, the more I had to say—and the more I thought my songs might be worth sharing. I saw that the lyrics resonated with my students, and I realized we're all kind of dealing with the same stuff here. I understood that the content of the lyrics needed to be talked about more than just once in a Bible study. So I started writing more songs to help me teach.

It is no coincidence that the first Casting Crowns single ever released ("If We Are The Body") is a direct product of my student ministry lessons.

Thirty years later, my songwriting is still the fruit of my work as a youth pastor. I've always said I'm a youth pastor first and Casting Crowns is second. No matter how well Casting Crowns has been received, I know for certain that we wouldn't exist without our ministry in the local church because Casting Crowns is the residual of those labors.

The first song I wrote for the "Only Jesus" album is called "One More Song For You." It's a praise song that emerged from my love of the local church and my desire to see The Great Commission fulfilled by each individual believer.

One day I looked down at the old piano in my house

and instantly remembered the song "East to West," which happened on that piano. "Praise You In This Storm" started on that piano. "Lifesong" started on that piano. "Who Am I" came to life right there on that piano. A flood of memories washed over me as I remembered these little worship times between just Jesus and me at that old piano—the intimate moments that, by his grace, turned into something I hear people sing back to me in other languages in venues around the world. Now *that* is an experience I can't put into words.

But I tried anyway.

It can be a little intimidating looking down at that piano sometimes. I'm human, so I feel the pressure. I know it's my flesh rearing its ugly head through pride and insecurity, but still sometimes I think, *How in the world am I going to do that again?* I feel a weird need to write songs as well as I did the last time, if not better, even though I recognize I'm not the one who came up with all the others. The pressure seems to weigh heavier every year.

Anytime I start feeling the pressure of whether Casting Crowns is going to be good enough to stay in people's worlds, I'm reminded of why I write in the first place. Steven Curtis Chapman said something to me when he and I started writing together on the song "Voice the Truth." Steven said Bill Gaither offered him advice when Steven was a young songwriter.

"Every song needs to be given the 'So What?' test," Bill told Steven. "At the end of it, you ask, 'So what?' Why does anybody need to hear what I'm saying? Why is this song here? Am I just adding to the noise, or do I have something to say that's going to point people to God?"

I think about that test every time I write. I refuse to be a songwriter for songwriting's sake. I'm not going to write songs just so we can have more songs, and, ironically, that's the main question that arises in "One More Song For You."

Is there still room for one more song?

Despite the intimidation of staring at that old piano, I knew the answer to my question. As long as I'm in the Word and soaking in God's truth, and as long as he's the Well that I draw from as I pour into people, he's going to have something to say through me.

So what started as an intimidating and even fearful moment became a question that was answered by this truth: I cannot coast. God still has a song for me to share, a truth for me to tell.

I can't let up, and here's why: I'll be onstage on a Saturday night on the other side of the country, telling the story behind "Voice of Truth," and God will use it to touch hearts while people sing. It's a huge God moment. But the teenagers in my student ministry have grown up with "Voice of Truth." They know it already. That hat is so old it's not even in the front of the closet.

So when I get home, my students are like, "Oh, that's cool. What else do you have?" It really keeps me in check. The local church doesn't have rock stars. These kids have grown up with me. They've known me since they were babies and they're not impressed anymore. They just know me as Mark, and I can't coast on something I said years ago. I have to keep growing.

In a unique way, "One More Song For You" led me to The Great Commission in Matthew 28:18-20. I've always seen discipleship as a command, and it is, because the last thing Jesus instructed us before he ascended to Heaven was to go make disciples. So I've always felt it was something any dutiful Christian has to obey.

Yet as I think about sitting down with one of my students, Brian—he and I are going through Philippians right now—I'm thankful for the opportunity to shepherd him. The more I've poured into students over the years, the more I've come to see discipleship as one of God's gifts to us. There's a growth that occurs in your new life when you spiritually matter to somebody else.

Some days I'm in the Word and I'm where I should be spiritually. I'm drawing from Jesus and I'm ready to charge Hell with a water pistol. And some days I'm tired and not in the mood and a little low, and I'd rather just coast for a few days so I can chill. But guess what? Brian is coming 3 p.m., and we're going to go through Philippians, ready or not.

Sure enough, Brian arrives at 3 p.m. We sit down, and I open the Word and start reading, and I'm like, "Oh my gosh, I needed to hear this. Thank you, Lord, for reminding me of this truth." The duty I wanted to escape is the very refreshment I needed.

Here am I am thinking I'm going to school Brian on Philippians when I read Paul say, "Man, it would be so much easier just to go to Heaven. I'm so tired. I'm so beaten up right now. I just want to be done with this, but I know that it's fruitful for you if I stay here. So I'm going to stay" (paraphrased from Philippians 1:19-26). Paul writes this to people he was discipling, and he wrote it with Timothy, his son in the faith.

When I share truth like that, not only is Brian learning but now I'm also encouraged and even rejuvenated.

God uses such moments to put a little gas in our tanks. I have had many days when I just wasn't hungry for the Word. I didn't want to worship. I didn't want to pray. I didn't want to read. I didn't want to do anything. I just wanted to be and let be so I could rest. But the accountability that comes with spiritually mattering to someone, with being his or her Paul, means I have to be available and engaged. In that moment of going knees to knees with someone, God fills me at the same time. What I saw only as a duty is really a personal blessing.

If we're willing to have one awkward moment to build a bridge to Jesus, we ought to be willing to invest our time to help others become bridge builders, too.

Every one of us needs a Paul who pours into us, but every one of us also needs a Timothy into whom we pour what we've learned. As long as we're pouring into somebody else, we're not stagnant. We're moving and growing.

And as long as I'm growing, I plan to sit down at that old piano, no matter how intimidated I feel. I plan to finger those keys until I play the melody I hear in my head. I plan to ask God to do what he did on my very first song and hold my hand. And I plan to listen until he gives me the words he wants me to sing, the words that lift only Jesus on high, the words to one more song for him.

## Chapter 12

# HOME
## PSALM 23

*The LORD is my shepherd; I shall not want. He makes me lie down in green pastures. He leads me beside still waters. He restores my soul. He leads me in paths of righteousness for his name's sake.*

*Even though I walk through the valley of the shadow of death, I will fear no evil, for you are with me; your rod and your staff, they comfort me.*

*You prepare a table before me in the presence of my enemies; you anoint my head with oil; my cup overflows. Surely goodness and mercy shall follow me all the days of my life, and I shall dwell in the house of the LORD forever.*

**PSALM 23 WELCOMES ME HOME.**

Its promises open the door to my hope. Its truths assure me that my Lord is ever present. Its words wrap me in rest. It promises me good.

Psalm 23 is the basis of a powerful worship song called

"Home," a spare ballad written by my friend, Joel Chandler, who helps lead worship for our Wednesday night student gatherings. I felt compelled to include it on the *Only Jesus* album because of how God uses its powerful lyrics in me personally. It slows me down. It reminds me of God's desire that I know him more.

I also noticed—again after the fact—that the title and substance of the song continued a theme God threaded throughout the *Only Jesus* album. The idea of *home* is referenced in several songs, including "Even When You're Running," "The Bridge," "One More Song For You," and, finally, "Home." They all convey the reality that Jesus has a voice that sounds like home, and he never stops calling out to those of us who are prone to wander or are weary and heavy-laden. He never stops saying, "Come to me." Psalm 23 is a "come to me" passage.

> **Because of the one who shepherds me, I can walk through the most treacherous of deep valleys and still not fear.**

I've heard and read Psalm 23 most of my life. It is so much more than funeral script. It features some of the simplest yet most profound word pictures in all of Scripture—beautiful, memorable words I can rest in. The psalmist leads me to a place where I'm lost in nothing but the Lord, the one who fills me to the point that I want not. The one who makes me lie down in the lush of green pastures and taste his fresh Living Water. The one who restores my soul when it is riddled with guilt and regret. Because of the one who shepherds me, I can walk through the most treacherous of deep valleys and still not fear. All of the faculties of the Almighty guard my life so that even in the face of death I am comforted. Psalm 23 isn't just sheer, eternal art; it is the power of God unto salvation.

And yet it includes a most curious line:

"You prepare a table before me in the presence of my enemies" (v. 5).

I've always skimmed through that verse to get to the next verses that resonated more deeply with me: He anoints my head with oil. My cup runs over. I'm going to dwell in the house of the Lord forever. I like the forever stuff. It means God's got me. I'm going to be OK.

It's wonderful that he prepares a table for me in front of people who don't like me, but what does that even mean?

Then one day I read through the verse again.

"You prepare a table for me in the presence of my enemies."

Something clicked. The verse reminded me of one of my favorite pursuits. I've always loved epic battle movies like *Star Wars*, *Gladiator*, *Braveheart*, and *Lord of the Rings*, all of which depict monumental war moments when armies are lined up to do battle. I'm not trying to go all Freud here, but perhaps those movies resonate with me at a deeper level because they remind me of times when I felt like all of Hell was coming against me. Looking back now, those moments don't seem as daunting. But during those scary times, it seemed as if the armies of the deep stood before me and I wondered if I would survive.

I correlate those life moments to what I've seen in the movies. In my darkest times, I've envisioned a wall of thousands of soldiers. They were all dark, armed, huge, and ominous. Their shadow was before them and behind them. It's like they were suspended in gloomy darkness while slamming the ground with their spears as battle trumpets blared, and I didn't see an end to the ocean of soldiers.

I thought, *There's no way out of this.* But whatever I faced that prompted such thoughts, I responded the only way I know how: "God, you've got to help me."

Now when I read that God prepares a table before me, I imagine myself standing in a huge field, pacing in the presence of my enemies as they take another step toward me. Another step. Another step. Their armor rattles, their horses neigh, their weapons clang together. Another step. Then another. They're picking up the pace.

And then Jesus shows up....

My first instinct would be to turn to everyone around and say, "Jesus is here. Watch this. No epic movie scene can compare with what he's about to do. I don't even know what he will do. Is he going to blow and dissolve them? Is he going to wave his arm and sweep them into dust? Will the ocean swallow them? What? What is he going to do? Surely he's going to get them good, and, finally, I'm going to get some justice here."

But all Jesus does is pull out a table and unfold its legs. He sets it up right there in the green pasture, trying to find an even spot because it's a little wobbly on one side. He steadies it and glances at me as I stumble through my words.

"Jesus, I don't know what to do. I need you. I'm so glad you're here. You've got to do something. They're here. The armies are here to get me."

Jesus doesn't flinch. He spreads a cloth over the table and smooths out the wrinkles. He pulls a small bag from around his neck. He reaches in the bag and pulls out a loaf of fresh bread and a plate and lays the bread on the plate. He takes out two cups and a bottle of wine and sets them on the table.

Well, I'm a Baptist, so it's grape juice. But on a day like this, I don't care what's in the bottle because I'm thinking, *Jesus, I'm going to die.*

I hear the armies take another step closer. Jesus is still looking down and arranging everything on the table, and I can feel the breath of the darkness on the back of my neck. All I can think is, *Jesus, if you don't do something right now I'm going down.*

Then Jesus looks up and says, "Have you tried this bread? There is a market on the city square. It has this little bakery, and if you go by there at just the right time in the morning, you can smell the bread oven for blocks. It's a sweet little lady and her husband. I just love it. You've got to try this."

"But, Jesus, they're right here. They're on us. I'm not going to make it. This will be my last meal. You have to do something."

Jesus picks up the bottle and fills the cups.

I can only imagine how maddening it would be to have this scene play out in real life—to know that Jesus showed up in answer to prayer but he showed up with a table. I've experienced so many times when I didn't just need him to show up. I needed him to show up exactly like I envisioned him showing up. I needed him to show up and do what I wanted him to do. I needed him to rescue me the way I wanted to be rescued. But he came a different way, and, in my mind, I just decided he never showed up. But he was there. Make no mistake. He was there.

> I needed him to rescue me the way I wanted to be rescued. But he came a different way.

If you have a chance to ask most atheists why they don't believe in God, and if you can get them past all their talking points and just ask them what happened, their stories are similar. Most of them will go back to a time when they really needed God to show up, and they don't think he did.

I've needed Jesus to fix things for me too. I've needed him to heal. I've needed him to make relationships right for me. I've needed him to deliver me from trials in a certain way. They didn't all end the way I thought they would. God didn't always work as I had hoped.

As I've matured, I now try to remember the table. I think of that army bearing down on me, their shields brushing against my back as I wait for the first cut to rip through my flesh. But then Jesus sits at the table. He never even glances over my shoulder. He breaks the bread, hands it to me, and smiles as he asks one simple question.

"Tell me, what was it that you were afraid of again?"

In reality, a Jesus who shows up to a battle with a sword is pretty amazing. But a Jesus who shows up to a battle and doesn't need a sword? And he doesn't need everything that I think he needs to be the victor and to rescue and to save? That Jesus is sovereign. That he sits me down and feeds me in front of everything that I would consider overwhelming and dark and hopeless displays his power more effectively than any other way I can imagine. That he is willing to prepare a table for me in my difficult times and in the presence of my darkest foes shows me that he is at perfect peace with the forces and trials that scare me to death. I can lay my anxious heart to rest when I'm with him.

A table says, "Let's sit a spell." A meal says, "Let's spend some time together. I want to get to know you more." Jesus doesn't mind setting a table in the middle of our battles because he knows he'll have our full attention.

When Jesus anoints my head with oil, it has a practical and symbolic meaning. People in ancient Palestine kept the polite custom of anointing their heads with oil at supper to help cover body odors from the day. They didn't have showers and body wash back then, so they made meals pleasant by washing feet and pouring aromatic oil into the hair to mask smells. The oil came to be associated with the gladness of good times.

Oil also is symbolic of the Holy Spirit throughout the Bible. I am regenerated when the Holy Spirit indwells me. When Jesus anoints my head with oil, it is emblematic of the promise and presence of the Holy Spirit, his salvation, and his work. In other words, Jesus identifies me with him through the anointing oil of the Holy Spirit.

I am his anointed one. And I sit at his table—a table *he* prepared for *me*. And he feeds me and gives me life and even gladness in the darkness and chaos.

Philippians 4:6-7 states, "Do not be anxious about anything, but in everything by prayer and supplication with thanksgiving let your requests be made known to God. And the peace of God, which surpasses all understanding, will guard your hearts and your minds in Christ Jesus."

I used to consider that verse ironic. If I'm anxious, be thankful? How can I be thankful when I'm anxious?

Psalm 23 gives the answer. I can sit at his table and say, "God, thank you that you're not anxious about this. Thank you that you are in control. Thank you for preparing my table before me. Thank you for anointing my head with your eternal oil."

And so I find my rest. I have nothing to fear.

In his presence, I am home.

For more individual copies or bulk orders of *Only Jesus*, please visit www.lifesongpublishing.com or www.castingcrowns.com.

**Also from Mark Hall with Tim Luke:**

*Lifestories*
*Your Own Jesus*
*The Well*
*Thrive*
*The Very Next Thing*

MARK HALL is the lead singer and songwriter for the GRAMMY Award-winning band Casting Crowns. He has been a student pastor for almost three decades, including 18 years at Eagle's Landing First Baptist Church in McDonough, Georgia. He and his wife, Melanie, have four children: John Michael, Reagan, Zoe, and Hope.

TIM LUKE serves as executive pastor of Eagle's Landing First Baptist Church, where he has been on staff for 19 years after serving as editor of In Touch magazine at In Touch Ministries in Atlanta. Tim and his wife, Karen, have two sons: Jacob and J.P.